Gary's warmth, knowledge, and experience shine through
this lively, fresh and inviting approach to conflict resolution.
He guides us through the rough waters of conflict to the joy
that comes when we connect deeper than our differences.
Gary, is truly a Warrior of the Heart in every way.

— Jerilyn Brusseau, Co-founder, PeaceTrees Vietnam

In language we can all understand and with situations we've all
suffered through, *Joy of Conflict* is a must for employees, managers,
parents and anyone who values their relationships with others.

— Paul Choudhury, P.Eng. Manager, System Control,
British Columbia Transmission Corporation

This book provides us with a new refreshing perspective,
presenting difficult concepts in a very "user friendly" way
which allows us to better understand the sources of conflict
around us, providing practical tools that can be put to use
by everyone. It is by far one of the best books
I've seen on workplace conflict.

— Jaylene Chew, Human Resources Professional

By using easy to relate to everyday stories, Gary encourages
us to move from being 'stuck' in our reoccurring patterns
of conflict. The opportunities to reflect and practice at the
end of each chapter makes learning new ways to
respond in conflict accessible to everyone.

— Pam White, Director, Centre for Conflict Resolution
Justice Institute of BC

Gary Harper's adroit use of the story-telling model and his common sense narrative approach casts a fresh perspective on the dynamics of conflict and is rich with the kind of insight that enhances problem-solving tool kits for organizations and individuals.

— Kevin Evans, Vice President, Western Canada,
Retail Council of Canada

This is a valuable read for anyone wanting a quick and accessible understanding of the conflict that has captured them and how to get out of it.

— Gerald Monk, author of *Narrative Mediation*

The Joy of Conflict manages to open doors to the world of conflict and conflict resolution with humor, creativity and insight. It's an adventure in reading and reflection that I would recommend to anyone who lives or works with anyone else.

— Michael Fogel, J.D., LL.B., M.Ed. (Counselling Psychology) former judge, presently a mediator and conflict resolution/leadership educator

The Joy of Conflict Resolution and its simple portrayal of victims, villains, and heroes has enabled me effectively address issues by being aware of the role I play during a conflict. Through Gary's illustrative humor, this book is an easy read and contains a wealth of information and tools on how to effectively deal with people. I think *The Joy of Conflict Resolution* would be a welcome addition to any technical support person's daily reading.

— George Young, MCSE
Bentall Capital, Manager, IT Infrastructure

Gary's story-telling approach transforms theory and experience into living colour. A wonderful approach of insight and skill development that I recommend without hesitation.

— Neil Godin, President, Neil Godin International Ltd.

The Joy of Conflict
RESOLUTION

Transforming
Victims, Villains
and Heroes
in the
Workplace
and at Home

GARY HARPER

NEW SOCIETY PUBLISHERS

Cataloguing in Publication Data:
A catalog record for this publication is available from the National Library of Canada.

Cover design and illustration by Diane McIntosh.
Illustrations by Derek Toye.

Printed in Canada by Friesens.
Eighth printing, January 2014.

New Society Publishers acknowledges the support of the Government of Canada through the Book Publishing Industry Development Program (BPIDP) for our publishing activities.

ISBN: 978-0-86571-515-8

Inquiries regarding requests to reprint all or part of *The Joy of Conflict Resolution* should be addressed to New Society Publishers at the address below.

To order directly from the publishers, please call toll-free (North America) 1-800-567-6772, or order online at www.newsociety.com
Any other inquiries can be directed by mail to:

New Society Publishers
P.O. Box 189, Gabriola Island, BC V0R 1X0, Canada
250-247-9737

New Society Publishers' mission is to publish books that contribute in fundamental ways to building an ecologically sustainable and just society, and to do so with the least possible impact on the environment, in a manner that models this vision. We are committed to doing this not just through education, but through action. We are acting on our commitment to the world's remaining ancient forests by phasing out our paper supply from ancient forests worldwide. This book is one step towards ending global deforestation and climate change. It is printed on acid-free paper that is **100% old growth forest-free** (100% post-consumer recycled), processed chlorine free, and printed with vegetable based, low VOC inks. For further information, or to browse our full list of books and purchase securely, visit our website at: www.newsociety.com

NEW SOCIETY PUBLISHERS   www.newsociety.com

*To the bridge builder and peacemaker
in each of us*

CONTENTS

ACKNOWLEDGMENTS

This book celebrates my community. While I may have authored the work, its content reflects the shared learning of the many friends, colleagues, and teachers with whom I have had the good fortune to dialogue over the years. The book draws also from what I have learned from thousands of my students while under the pretense that I was teaching them.

When the student is ready, the teacher will appear. Three teachers appeared to support and influence my personal and professional growth. Bob Trask opened the world of spirituality to me. Michael Fogel imparted the conflict resolution skills and principles that allowed me to make this field my profession. And Danaan Parry deepened my understanding of conflict by awakening the warrior of the heart within me.

Other colleagues shared more specific knowledge. Ken Cloke introduced me to the concept of the drama triangle and encouraged me to develop it. Lloyd Kornelsen turned me on to Jon Scieszka's *The True Story of the Three Little Pigs*. Camilla Witt shared her metaphor of "the knife going in". Joan Goldsmith, Bernie Mayer, Gerald Monk, and Maureen Fitzgerald graciously offered both their subject knowledge and their experience as authors.

The "not-quite-ready for prime-time players" of Turm-Oil Inc. gave up a Sunday afternoon to role play and develop the characters to whom you hopefully will relate. Thanks, Tim Chizik, Clare Connolly, Gloria Hamade, Terry Harris, and Carla Reiger.

Many others took time to brainstorm scenarios, review incarnations of the manuscript, and provide invaluable feedback: Ken Bellemare, Laurence Betts, Alice Caton, Ardyth Cooper, Barbara Densmore, Dennis Hilton, Margaretha Hoek, Tim Langdon, Michelle LeBaron, Julie MacFarlane, Ron Ohmart, Kathleen Tribe, and George and Edna Young. Other colleagues who willingly shared their experiences and wisdom are included in the book's final chapter.

The writing process itself was jump-started by my coach, Linda Dobson-Sayer, who helped me find my voice. My editor, Naomi Pauls, focused and tidied the work, encouraged me at each step, and kept my writing honest with her gentle "cliché alerts." Illustrator Derek Toye brought the characters to life and added a light touch to a potentially serious subject.

I was fortunate to work with New Society Publishers — only two ferry rides from home. Chris and Judith Plant freely offered their hospitality, support and experience. Ingrid Witvoet and Diane Killou polished the manuscript, and Heather Wardle and Diane McIntosh brought their creative energy and talents to the cover design. It seems only fitting that we collaborated so effectively to produce a book on the topic.

Closer to home, my parents, David and Enid Harper, imparted their love of learning and appreciation of the written word. I was fortunate to inherit my late father's creativity and a gentle cheekiness that I hope found its way into the work. I also benefited from my mother's precision and eagle-eyed proofreading of the manuscript.

My wife, Kathleen, and daughter, Shannon, have provided me with years of support and opportunities to practice conflict resolution. They also allowed me to share some of our timeless moments with you in the pursuit of learning.

Thank you all.

— Gary Harper, March 2004

INTRODUCTION

"*The Joy of Conflict Resolution*? You've got to be kidding," I thought when a colleague suggested the title during a brainstorming session. Where is the joy in conflict? Most people avoid it or deal with it reluctantly, as a necessary evil. Yet when Chris Plant at New Society resurrected this title from the brainstorm scrap heap, I reconsidered as I recalled the satisfaction and freedom I experienced when I had resolved a conflict or assisted others to.

At work or at home, conflict is a part of life. How do we respond? Sometimes we suppress it by avoiding people, leaving jobs or ending relationships. When that isn't an option, we may nurse grudges until we can't stand it anymore, at which time we may explode and engage in fruitless and even embarrassing confrontations. Unresolved conflict takes its toll on us and on our relationships. We can all learn to resolve it better.

In what follows, you'll be invited to examine conflict stories. By identifying the ever-changing roles people play in conflict, you will be able to understand and resolve differences. Many people in conflict feel hopelessly stuck. And the harder they push or pull, the deeper they sink, locked into viewing conflicts in terms of right and wrong, good and bad. Without realizing it, they had entered a "drama triangle" populated by victims, villains and heroes. Trapped in a world of winners and losers they find collaboration impossible.

The Joy of Conflict Resolution uses the drama triangle to illustrate patterns of conflict and to identify the roles people play. You will learn basic skills to help you create more productive roles, move beyond the drama triangle and resolve conflicts collaboratively. You will see how curiosity uncovers the other side of the story, how empathy builds bridges and how assertion separates the person from the problem.

You will learn what fairy tales and Hollywood movies have to teach us about conflict. You'll also be a fly on the wall at Turm-Oil Inc. and follow the exploits of its employees as they encounter sticky situations everyone will relate to. You might even think the examples have been lifted from your own workplace or family! Each chapter also provides an opportunity to apply the concepts and skills to conflicts in your own lives.

The ideas presented in this book appear simple at face value, yet can lead to profound realizations. As you are challenged to broaden your perspectives, you will discover previously unseen possibilities for resolution. Conflict might be uncomfortable, but it produces energy. We can choose what we do with that energy. Every conflict provides the opportunity for learning, growth, and enhanced relationships. In seizing that opportunity lies *The Joy of Conflict Resolution*.

I hope you'll join me.

CHAPTER 1

VICTIMS, VILLAINS, AND HEROES

*A villain is a misunderstood hero; a hero is a
self-righteous villain.*

Fairy tales of conflict

As a child, snuggled under your bedcovers, you probably drifted
off to sleep to a story along these lines:

> Once upon a time, in a galaxy far, far away, there lived
> a beautiful princess. One day, she dared to wander from
> the safety of the palace and was captured by an evil
> dragon. A noble, selfless prince sallied forth to rescue
> the princess. He journeyed far and wide and at long last
> found the dragon in his lair. After a fierce battle, he was
> able to slay the dragon and rescue the princess. The
> prince and princess ultimately married and, of course,
> lived happily ever after.

In today's workplace, you might have heard an updated version of
this tale in the coffee room:

> Once upon a time, in a galaxy far too close to home,
> there lived an innocent, hardworking employee. One
> day, she dared to wander from the safety of her cubicle
> and speak out during a department meeting. She was

immediately attacked and berated by her evil manager and embarrassed in front of all. A noble, selfless shop steward sallied forth to aid the poor employee. He journeyed far and wide through the grievance procedure and at long last trapped the manager with a harassment complaint. After a fierce battle, the shop steward was able to vanquish the evil manager and his human resources minion and ensure justice was served for the employee. She and the shop steward ultimately left the company and, of course, lived happily ever after.

If you'd had lunch with the manager and his human resources advisor, however, you would have heard a quite different version:

Once upon a time, in yet another galaxy, there lived an innocent, hardworking manager. One day, plagued by downsizing and re-engineering, he dared to wander from the safety of his office and meet with his employees. He was greeted by an angry mob who demanded things over which he had no control. The manager battled against all odds to quell the mob and solve their problems until he was blindsided by an irate (and obviously unbalanced) employee and her shop steward henchman. After a fierce battle, and with the help of his ally, the company's human resources advisor, the manager saved the day and ensured the success of his department. The victory, alas, was not without a price, as the noble manager suffered a harassment charge to the heart. From that day forward, his scar reminded him to trust no employee.

We all have our tales of conflict. We complain at one time or another about controlling spouses, lazy co-workers, or Attila the Hun bosses. We never seem to tire of recounting the injustices that have befallen us and bad-mouthing those who have "done it to us." This black and white view of life may be satisfying, but when applied to a conflict it is unlikely to lead to resolution. When we paint ourselves as the innocent victim and view the other person as the enemy, we become locked in a power struggle complete with anger and frustration.

The fairy tales and myths of our childhood impact us more than we realize. They present larger-than-life characters and a simplistic world of good and evil. Not surprisingly, we relate to the characters in these stories and may even subconsciously view the world in their terms.

Try putting the words "Once upon a time" in front of one of your conflict stories. Through this lens you can broaden your perspective on the conflict, identify your role in it, and choose a more constructive and collaborative way to resolve it. Although this approach lacks much of the drama and excitement of traditional competitive ones, it produces richer, more lasting resolution and maintains relationships. Let's have a look at the roles we typically take on in the mythic "drama triangle."

Roles we play

In classic tales, we consistently encounter three types of characters: the victim (often represented as a damsel in distress or an innocent youth); the villain (a witch, giant, or dragon); and the hero (the white knight or prince). Although these character types originate in fairy tales and myths, we encounter them also on the front pages of our newspapers, on our favorite television shows, and on movie screens everywhere. No wonder we see conflict in the same way.

Traditionally, the villain captures or controls the damsel, who ultimately is rescued by the prince (as in "Snow White"). Sometimes the victim becomes the hero ("Popeye" cartoons spring to mind). Other times, the villain is transformed through forgiveness (Darth Vader in "Star Wars," for example). However the drama plays out, these character types will be front and center.

Because we experience our own conflicts as stories, we unconsciously adopt these roles. Most often, we see ourselves as the victim — innocent and powerless. Sometimes, we play the hero and risk the discomfort of conflict to right the wrong and see justice done. And, very occasionally, we even may slip into the role of the villain, venting our anger or frustration on another person. Each role provides a limited perspective on the conflict. Together, they form a "drama triangle."

Of course, each person in the conflict has their own story. Our adversaries likely see themselves as the victim and paints us as the villain. We, in turn, expend tremendous energy to defend ourselves and our reputation from such an unfair label. It's no wonder, then, that we view conflict as negative. We experience the pain of "being hit," the outrage of being unfairly labeled as the villain, and the stress of needing to defend ourselves. Not a pleasant combination.

We can change this if we are willing to acknowledge how easily we slip into the roles of the drama triangle. With this awareness, we can choose to view and approach our conflicts differently. We can see the other not as the villain but as someone with whom we must work to identify and solve the problem. By doing so, we move beyond the drama triangle and toward resolution.

THE VICTIM

In a conflict, each person feels hit first.

We experience conflict as an attack on our self-esteem or ego. We may see our values threatened or fear someone will deprive us of something we desire or need. We feel victimized — and blame someone or something else.

The victim role includes a sense of powerlessness. We often withdraw — the "flight" part of "fight or flight" — or become passive. We may even freeze like a deer caught in the headlights. We wait for something to change or for someone to rescue us. (Remember Rapunzel, trapped in her tower.) Although some of us suffer in silence, many of us express our frustration by complaining about the situation and blaming the person we see as responsible for our plight (the villain).

Victimhood has its rewards. We receive a significant amount of attention in the form of sympathy. If we are really lucky, we may even attract a hero to sally forth against our villain and "right the wrong" for us. Alternatively, we can play the "guilt card" in the hope that the other person will see the pain they have caused, recognize

the error of their ways, and behave differently. But even if we successfully manipulate another into doing what we want, the accom-
panying resentment often poisons relationships.

By playing the victim, we also absolve ourselves of responsibility.
After all, we are innocent and the conflict is not our fault. Rather
than meeting the situation head-on, we justify inaction by telling
ourselves that the other person is the one who needs to change. It
seems safer (and less messy) for us to ignore or avoid the conflict or
to snipe from a distance.

The rewards of victimhood come at a price. As victims, we relinquish our sense of control or influence over the situation. This sense
of powerlessness erodes our self-esteem and leads to resentment and
frustration. Others may see us as weak or needy, and our relationships may become defined by co-dependency. In short, by playing
the victim we trade personal power for sympathy and ironically
increase the very stress and negativity we seek to avoid.

On a more positive note, the victim role reflects our goodness,
sensitivity, and compassion. The victim/princess in stories seldom
seeks revenge, but often facilitates reconciliation through unwaver-
ing love and forgiveness. (Cinderella's continued good cheer toward
her vain and envious stepsisters is a prime example of this.) These
qualities are essential to allow us to escape the drama triangle and
adopt a more cooperative approach to our conflicts.

THE HERO

> *I've stands all I can stand and I can't stands no more.*
>
> — *Popeye the Sailor Man*

The typical plot line of a Popeye cartoon features Popeye taking
abuse from the villainous Bluto. Eventually, Popeye reaches the limit
of his considerable patience, pops open his can of spinach, and
administers Bluto the beating he so justly deserves. And all is well
with the world.

Though we initially experience conflict as the victim (if only for a
split second), we often shift to hero mode to protect ourselves,

defend our interests, and even the score. This role represents courage and action, selflessness and nobility. The hero ventures forth to do what must be done — justice will be its own reward. The role represents the part of us that is noble and courageous, that will step forward, take a stand, and risk discomfort or judgment.

There is a darker side to the hero role, however. That is the fine line between righteousness and self-righteousness. What we may see as clever, others may see as manipulative. What we see as taking charge, others may experience as controlling. In rescuing the damsel, the hero usually attacks, slays, or captures the villain. When we agree that the hero's cause is just, we condone and even applaud what are clearly aggressive behaviors. We can even justify our own aggressive and hurtful behavior by telling ourselves, "They had it coming."

Based on actions alone, a hero is simply a self-righteous villain. In a different context, Robin Hood would have done five to ten years of hard time for extortion and armed robbery. Instead, his actions are not only excused but also revered in legend because of his noble cause and earlier mistreatment by the evil Sheriff. Similarly, Jack (of "Jack and the Beanstalk" fame) made his reputation through trespass and burglary, though these acts are seen as heroic because the giant was mean. You get the drift.

Some of us may even involve ourselves in the conflicts of others as self-appointed heroes — to fix the problem for them. Though our intentions may be noble, this approach reinforces the helplessness of the victim we are rescuing and further entrenches the other person in the villain role — thus unwittingly perpetuating the conflict (and the drama).

THE VILLAIN

Now you know what it feels like.

We see villains as hateful, bitter, and evil. Villains traditionally capture and control the victim for their own purposes or deprive the victim of something. This role represents the side of us that can be petty, mean-spirited, and vindictive (what "Star Wars" calls the "dark side" of the Force). This dark side includes the part of us that is mistrustful, controlling, and fearful. The villain acts aggressively, attacking and hurting others and taking what they want. Many of these behaviors center on control. When we experience someone controlling us, we quickly cast them as the villain in our conflict story.

In fact, the behaviors of the villain are similar to those of the hero, distinguished only by how we judge them. Internationally, the same acts of violence we condemn as terrorism are seen by other ideologies as the selfless acts of freedom fighters. Arnold Schwarzenegger's Terminator character was listed by the American Film Institute as one of the top 100 villains of all time for his role in "The Terminator" and also as one of the top 100 heroes for his appearance in "Terminator 2: Judgment Day." It all depends whose side you're on.

In our conflict stories, we judge the villain's cause to be wrong or unworthy and accordingly judge their actions to be evil. Yet looking strictly at behavior, a villain is simply a misunderstood hero. Even people who act inappropriately or antisocially have their story, in which they see themselves as victims and justify their actions as "evening the score." One person's justice is another's revenge.

For the bad rap the villain role receives, it does embody positive qualities. The villain usually is patient. Myths and fantasy tales (such as *The Lord of the Rings*) are filled with stories of evil forces that lurk for a thousand years, awaiting the opportunity to re-emerge and seek revenge. Lord Voldemort in the Harry Potter series is another notable example of perseverance, albeit for an evil purpose. The villain also represents creativity and ingenuity, though we probably would call these traits manipulative or sneaky. The key to resolving conflict collaboratively is to apply our patience and creativity to solving the problem, not to exacting revenge on the other person.

Beyond the drama triangle

Every search for a hero begins with a villain.

— *"Mission Impossible 2"*

All three types of characters in our conflict stories require each other in order to exist — they form a "drama triangle." We cannot see ourselves as a victim without casting the other person as a villain. Before we can shift to hero mode, we must have a wrong to right — a foe to vanquish. Who better than the villain? Similarly, a hero needs someone to rescue. (Sometimes, that someone might be ourselves.)

FIGURE 1A
THE DRAMA TRIANGLE

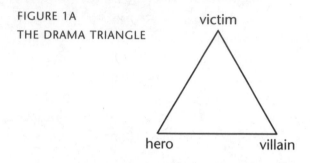

As long as we see ourselves as victims or heroes, we automatically create villains in our conflicts. Not surprisingly, when we see (and treat) someone as a villain, they in turn feel victimized by us — and see us as the villain. Behaviors we consider self-defense, they experience as attacks and further evidence we cannot be trusted. And the walls of judgment and justification are buttressed on both sides.

So we can see that the roles we play in our conflicts continually shift. It's not uncommon for someone to feel attacked (as victim), defend themselves (as hero), and, in their anger, attempt to inflict as much punishment as possible on their attacker (as villain). This can happen within seconds!

Our conflicts consequently are populated by a rotating cast of victims, villains, and heroes. While this undoubtedly leads to excellent drama and excitement, it seldom leads to resolution. The challenge is to step beyond the drama triangle, yet utilize the positive characteristics of each role to work with the other person to identify and solve the problem. To eliminate villains from our conflicts, we must be prepared to give up being a victim (and the sympathy and apparent safety the role offers). We also need to relinquish the mantle of the hero (and the self-righteousness that accompanies this role).

The drama triangle and its roles inevitably produce a win-lose approach to conflict. One person wins; the other must lose. No one likes to lose, and we will battle ferociously to avoid defeat. Even when one person loses the battle, the war is seldom over. The loser continues to seek justice and retribution. Revenge, however subtly, underlies conflict stories and ultimately leads to a lose-lose situation.

CASTING NEW ROLES

Let's examine how we can shift our perspective and approach to allow resolution in which both people get what they need and there are no losers.

To set aside the role of victim is more easily said than done. We begin by being accountable for our feelings and reactions in conflict. We do not have to deny or devalue our feelings or needs, but must accept responsibility for them. After all, whose problem is it if you go home frustrated with your boss at the end of a workday? Who "owns" the problem? (Hint: your boss may be sleeping like a baby as you lie awake endlessly replaying the events of the day.)

Consider the difference between the statements "You never make time for my issues at meetings" and "I'm frustrated that we didn't discuss the budget during the meeting". The first statement is loaded with blame and judgment, casts the other person as the villain, and holds them responsible for how we feel. The second shares information, takes responsibility for feelings, and begins to identify the problem to be discussed and resolved.

Similarly, we can ask directly for what we need instead of quietly complaining to others about our plight. Asking is both uncomfortable and empowering. It's uncomfortable because we can no longer blame others and refuse to change, empowering because we become an active participant in shaping our life. To reap the rewards of assertiveness, we have to risk the discomfort of confronting a person or problem.

The role of hero can be as unproductive as that of victim in resolving conflict. This self-righteous mindset condones our attack on the villain as justice. Attack is met with counterattack; the conflict persists and usually escalates. Our ego fuels our need to be right and we become attached to a specific outcome. At this point, the conflict often becomes a power struggle.

We can address and resolve conflict much more productively if we let go of the need to be "right" and focus instead on ways to get our needs met. This focus opens up possibilities we might otherwise ignore. The energy devoted to a win-lose power struggle can instead be applied to problem solving. This approach often is referred to as "separating the people from the problem."

This in no way means we should give in or avoid an issue just to keep the peace. We need to exhibit a hero's courage in different ways: to raise an issue directly rather than to attack; to enter the uncomfortable place we experience as conflict and to stay present; to listen to things we may disagree with; to see the conflict through to real resolution. We need to stand up for ourselves in a way that doesn't knock the other person down. We must shift our judgment to curiosity and our self-righteousness to openness — much more easily said than done.

There is a fine line between the roles of hero and villain, and in conflict we can easily and unconsciously slip into the role of villain. When we attack another person (even in self-defense) and attempt to hurt them in some way, we have become the villain. Fueled by anger or frustration, we may come out with statements such as "I don't care what you think" and "Don't be such a jerk." We may even "lose it" and exhibit the very behaviors (threatening, interrupting, swearing) we find so objectionable in others. We victimize the other person anew and perpetuate the attack-defend cycle.

Although others may see us as a villain, we can change their view if we are willing to relinquish our need to control. No one likes being controlled. When we feel controlled by another, we experience the other person as "difficult" and label them as a villain. Since we resent being controlled, why should we expect other people to react any differently?

Abandoning the need to control is a good news/bad news scenario. When we relinquish our need for control, we make room for fresh and creative possibilities to resolve our conflicts and even redefine our relationships. At the same time, we have to give up our need to be right. (I never said it would be easy.)

When we view the conflict as a challenge or problem to solve, we allow collaboration. We can remain "hard on the problem" yet "soft on the people."

FROM ADVERSARIES TO PARTNERS

When we live on the drama triangle, we see the other person as our adversary — the villain. If only they would change, we reason, things would be fine. They stand between us and happiness. Ironically, they usually are thinking the same thing about us. To resolve conflict, we need to relinquish our roles as victim, villain, and hero and work with the other person to solve the problem. If we need a villain, let it be the problem, not the person. The diagram below symbolizes this shift — from the drama triangle to the circle of resolution.

FIGURE 1B
THE CIRCLE OF RESOLUTION

THE CIRCLE OF RESOLUTION

Interestingly, the circle and triangle intersect not at the three corners of the triangle but in the middle on each side. Similarly, we must meet the other person in the middle. This doesn't mean "splitting the difference." It means telling them our story (in a way they will be able to hear it) and listening to their story with curiosity. Such open communication fosters mutual understanding. This understanding provides a bridge over which we can exit the drama triangle and enter the circle of resolution.

Summary

In a conflict, each person feels hit first. We initially experience conflict as the victim of an attack or threat. This role is accompanied by
a sense of innocence and powerlessness.

The roles of hero and villain both exhibit aggressive behaviors
and are distinguished only by our judgment of what is right or just.

To resolve conflict, we need to relinquish our roles as victim, villain, and hero and work with the other person against the problem.

From theory to practice

Consider a conflict in which you are or were involved. Examine your
perspective on the conflict with respect to the roles of the drama triangle.

- When did you first feel like the victim?
- When might the other person have first felt like the victim?
- If you're feeling brave, tell your conflict story to a friend, have
  them pretend to be the other person, and ask them to tell the
  story from the other perspective. Monitor your reaction as
  you hear yourself cast as the villain.

CHAPTER 2

LESSONS FROM THE SANDBOX

All I need to learn about conflict I learned in kindergarten.

Grow up, already

"I feel like I'm running a daycare around here," complains a weary manager. "They're acting like a couple of kids," opines an exasperated co-worker. "I wish he'd stop pouting and deal with this in a mature way," says a frustrated supervisor.

We often describe people in conflict as "acting like children." Although such a comparison does a disservice to children and their ability to cooperate (most of the time), it can provide us with clues about what underlies conflicts in our workplaces and homes.

We learn to play our parts on the drama triangle at such an early age that we do it unconsciously. As outlined in Chapter 1, the drama triangle provides attention and sympathy for the victim, admiration for the hero, and contempt for the villain. Many of the behaviors we develop as children and carry forward in life reflect our desire to avoid being cast as the villain and to be seen instead as the victim. After all, if we can stake out the moral high ground of being the victim, others normally will see us as innocent, sympathize with our plight, and comfort us. We also learn from a young age about the judgment and guilt that flow from being seen as the villain.

My PhD advisor can beat up your PhD advisor

During a conversation about various schoolyard themes that play out in the adult world, a friend and I were discussing "My dad can beat up your dad." He recounted his experience of a dinner at a national conflict resolution conference. Two experts were debating their respective theories about conflict. Within minutes, curiosity had evaporated and dialogue was replaced by a heated argument over the merits of their approaches. The focus quickly shifted to the credentials of their respective PhD advisors and which one carried more weight. How ironic that two "experts" in the field of conflict resolution, confronted by a challenge to the validity of their work, so quickly reverted to an adult version of "My dad can beat up your dad."

Why would these two men of learning revert so quickly to behavior most of us associate with playground squabbles? One reason is habit. As children they learned coping behaviors for conflict, and while these may have become more sophisticated as they matured, old habits die hard. Second, they were stuck on the drama triangle. They both fought to bolster their credibility so they would be seen as the hero, defending what is "right." Their identities were attached to having their theory accepted as "right." Perhaps we really do teach what we need to learn.

Themes from the playground

I recently visited friends and their two young daughters, aged two and four. Under the pretense of entertaining the kids, I grabbed a crayon and gleefully began coloring with them. It wasn't long before the elder girl noticed her sister with a dark-green crayon and declared, "I need that one." When I attempted to distract her and avoid the brewing conflict, she turned her attention to my crayon. "I need the blue one," she asserted. In the interests of peace, I gave her the blue crayon and picked up a red one. You can guess what happened next — the red crayon was now indispensable for her. It soon became a game. She would watch as I contemplated the next crayon I needed. When I chose one, the predictable "*That's* the one I need" followed. It was clear to the amused spectators that this wasn't really about the crayons but rather was an expression of the child's independence.

Conflict among grown-ups can be equally symbolic, yet we often get mesmerized by the "crayons" and miss the root of the conflict. Of course, sometimes, as Freud acknowledged, "a cigar is just a cigar" and conflict is about just what it appears to be about. These conflicts are relatively easy to solve. Other times, however, we are so concerned with judging who is right that we overlook the real issue. We treat the symptoms and ignore the cause. This accounts for the times we seemingly "solve" a problem, only to have it recur in a slightly different form, or for the times people react out of all proportion to what seems to be a simple, routine matter.

To help us understand and resolve conflict, let's examine a few basic "playground" themes and how they present themselves in the adult world.

You're not the boss of me (independence)

A group of kids are playing tag at the local playground when one touches another with a triumphant "You're it." The other immediately responds, "Am not! I was touching home base." The first counters, "You have to have both feet in the square. You're it." The second, outraged at this injustice, refuses to knuckle under. "Who died and left you in charge, bossy-pants?" he blurts as he sticks out his tongue, jumps on his bike, and pedals away.

A mom shakes her head as she surveys her teenager's room. She could swear she saw something move in the pile of clothes and papers under the bed. Exasperated, she yells down the hall over the sound of the blaring music to her daughter, "For the hundredth time, clean up that room." The teen rolls her eyes and shouts back, "It's my room. I'll keep it the way I want."

The new controller has just finished showing the management team a three-page, color-coded expense account form and insists that it be completed within 24 hours of a trip. The sales manager shakes his head in disbelief and says, "Where do you get off telling me how to run my department? We've got better things to do than spend all day on your petty paperwork."

Underlying these examples of "You're not the boss of me" is an *independence* theme. We need to feel some degree of control over our lives and surroundings. If we feel powerless in some areas, we often will find other issues on which to take a stand. This explains why employees may file grievance over what management sees as insignificant issues. Employees who feel they have little say about their working environment often will find relatively minor issues on which to take a stand.

GAME'S CLOSED — YOU CAN'T PLAY (BELONGING)

A young boy, sporting his favorite team jersey, breathlessly pedals to the park to join the neighborhood basketball game. He is immediately told, "Game's closed. Go away." When he protests, he's told, "This is for the big kids. Go play with the little kids." Smoldering, he begins to shoot at one of the hoops, disrupting the game and incurring the wrath and threats of the other kids. Outsized and outnumbered, he leaves, dreaming of the day when he'll be big enough to rule the court.

A new student sits down at a table in the high school cafeteria. Without so much as a hello, one of the other students says, "You can't sit here. This is for club members only." "What club?" the new student asks expectantly. "The one you're not a member of," smirks the other to the guffaws of the rest. The red-faced intruder moves to another table.

A long-term employee appears at the door of the human resources manager to file a grievance for harassment. She complains that two male colleagues have refused to acknowledge her "good morning" since a heated exchange at a recent team meeting. She is angered by what she sees as shunning.

The anxiety people feel when beginning a new job may stem more from office politics than from their job duties. With whom do we have coffee? Where do we fit? How do we find our place in this new environment?

Belonging and *inclusion* are basic human needs, and when they are denied or threatened we react. We feel victimized and perceive those who exclude us as villains. This theme shows up in the many variations of "us vs. them" that play out in organizations: regional vs. head office; union vs. management; suits vs. the floor; new hires vs. long-term employees.

THAT'S NO FAIR — HER PIECE IS BIGGER THAN MINE (RECOGNITION)

A father returns home from a business trip and is swarmed by his two young sons in anticipation of the traditional "What did you bring me?" gift. He presents each of them with a toy double-decker bus from London — identical except for color. One is red, the other blue. The younger of the two gleefully begins playing with his new blue bus. The elder scowls, looks reproachfully at Dad, and says (yes, you guessed it), "How come he gets the blue one? That's no fair!"

A teenager primps before the mirror before escaping from home for a Saturday evening with the gang. When the parent dutifully reminds them of their midnight curfew, they glower and say (yes, you guessed it again), "That's no fair. You let Jamie stay out until 1:00."

Two employees chew the fat over vending machine coffee in the plant lunchroom. The subject of a recent job reclassification arises. "I can't believe those guys on the loading docks got bumped up to a Level 6. We have to have a two-year certificate and they can just walk in off the street. Why are we still a Level 4?"

On the surface, these conflicts seem to be about fairness, though if we look deeper we can see that respect and *recognition as an individual* often underlie disputes over money, rules, and resources. If we feel we get the short end of things, we fear we are not valued.

It's hard to see the picture when you're in the frame

Many times we fail to resolve a conflict because we fail to identify the real issue. We are so anxious to fix things that we treat the symptoms and ignore the root cause. This is particularly true where conflict recurs in slightly different forms, all reflecting a common theme. If you experience this type of situation, stand back and ask yourself questions such as the following:

- If it weren't about the [corner office] what might it really be about?

- What might this person fear?
- What might this issue symbolize?
- What is the theme of this conflict?

Asking such questions allows us to probe for the source of the conflict. Some people say, "The problem named is the problem solved." While resolving conflict might not be quite that easy, identifying the problem allows us to focus our time and effort on the real issue and not be distracted by red herrings. This approach often will uncover valuable information and previously untapped possibilities. There are many ways to provide recognition, for example, once it is identified as the root need.

Conflict as its own reward

Imagine you supervise a production line at an industrial bakery. On one side of the conveyor, workers fold the croissants in a certain way (say, left over right). Workers on the other side of the conveyor, however, are adamant that it is better to fold the croissants right over left. When you investigate, you find that neither approach impacts efficiency, quality, or safety. Yet you find your production line divided literally down the middle. The groups have ceased speaking to each other, tension hangs in the air, and grievances begin to trickle to your desk.

As supervisor you will know that one side of the production line averages 15 years of service with your company; workers on the other side have all been hired within the past two years. The two sides also represent different ethnic groups.

Examine the situation from the perspective that "all behavior makes sense." What are these individuals getting *during* the conflict? By simply being on the drama triangle, they receive:

- an opportunity to exercise *independence* as they play the hero and stand up to the villain. This way of exerting power often underlies conflict in situations where those involved have routine and regimented jobs, with little sense of control.
- a feeling of *belonging*. They banded together to oppose the villains. By creating a "them," they created an "us."

- *recognition* or attention. The drama they created certainly attracted attention from both management and co-workers. Employees commonly feel ignored by management (unless, of course, something goes wrong). Conflict provides long-overdue attention and recognition.

These motivators are *identity needs.* Note that they are the same needs that underlie the "schoolyard" themes discussed earlier. Our baggage from forgotten schoolyard conflicts explains why we are triggered by certain behaviors, yet take other behaviors in stride.

Ironically, these same identity needs also are fulfilled by membership on a successful team. With membership come purpose, inclusion, and recognition. Organizations whose culture does not value these identity needs risk getting mired in conflict as employees seek other ways to fill these needs. As Fram Oil Filters tells car owners, "You can pay me now or pay me later."

As the supervisor in the croissant-folding controversy, you would not resolve the conflict by simply dictating a certain procedure. Resolution would require that those involved have an opportunity to tell their story and express their needs. By listening to both sides at a deeper level, you probably would learn that the apparent problem was but a symptom of deeper concerns.

So remember that conflict can exist at different levels. Where it is repetitive and seems petty, its roots probably lie at a deeper level. Any resolution must recognize and address the underlying concerns.

The roots of defensiveness

From an early age we learn that it can be a "dog-eat-dog world." As we take some hits along the way, we naturally develop strategies to defend ourselves. Over time, these survival techniques become habits. We develop automatic responses to conflict and may, through years of practice, even elevate defensiveness to an art form.

These basic "playground" defenses reflect our attempts to claim or avoid certain roles on the drama triangle. In conflict, we frequently feel blamed and personally attacked. This feeling inevitably triggers defensiveness, as we refuse to accept being painted as the villain and will do almost anything to escape that role. We quickly learn to scramble to the safety associated with the moral high ground of the victim. After all, as the victim we must be innocent. Of course, this casts the other person as the villain and creates an ongoing cycle of defensiveness and counterattack. Entertaining and exhilarating, perhaps, but in the end stressful and draining.

FIGURE 2A
SCRAMBLING TO BE THE VICTIM,
REFUSING TO BE THE VILLAIN

victim

hero   villain

Chapter 10 explores different types of defensive behavior and provides strategies to manage each.

Summary

The surface issues in a conflict may obscure the underlying source of the dispute. Where conflict is repetitive and seems petty, its roots probably lie deeper. We may be so anxious to fix the problem that we treat only the symptoms. Any resolution must recognize and address the underlying concerns, which often involve independence, belonging, or recognition.

Conflict on the drama triangle is marked by two dominant dynamics: people refuse to be cast as the villain in another's story and subsequently scramble to gain the moral high ground of being the victim.

From theory to practice

Consider either a repetitive conflict in your life or one that occurred over something you considered petty. Ask yourself the following questions:

- If it weren't about the [surface issue] what might it really be about?
- What is the theme of this conflict?

CHAPTER 3

JUST LIKE THE MOVIES

In a story, nothing moves but for conflict.
— Screenwriter's adage

Elements of conflict stories

Stories consist of three basic elements: plot, characters, and theme. The theme brings the characters into some form of conflict: with each other, with themselves, or with nature. Take the story from Chapter 1 as an example. The employee who was chastised by her boss might tell her story to a friend like this:

> You won't believe what's going on at work. They brought in a new manager and he's already turning things upside down. He never even bothered to ask us — or he would have found out we already tried these things and they flat out didn't work. When he finally asked what we thought, I told him. Then he accused me of being "negative." I was so ticked off I told him he was a joke as a manger and almost walked out of the meeting. I finally had to see my staff rep. This jerk isn't going to make me the fall guy for his incompetence.

Even this short and simple story has its plot, characters, and conflict theme. Let's look at each.

THE PLOT

A story's plot provides the framework for the events as they unfold. It consists of what the characters say and do: their words and actions. The plot in a person's conflict story reflects their perception of the facts. The plot of the employee's story would consist of what she saw and heard:

- She has a new manager
- The new manager changed several procedures
- She was not consulted about the changes
- She told the new manager at a meeting that they had tried those things before without success
- The manager said she was being negative
- She contacted her shop steward, etc.

Words and actions are objective; perspectives, recollections, and interpretations vary even at the best of times. Ask witnesses to a crime to recount what happened and you likely will get as many variations as there are witnesses. No one sees the entire picture, especially in conflict, where emotions produce tunnel vision. To broaden our perspective, we need to encourage the other person to share their story. What happened from their perspective? We may uncover information that helps us make sense of what otherwise seemed irrational or hurtful behavior. As challenging as it may be to entertain the possibility of a different perspective on our conflicts, it is even more difficult to muster the self-control to hear another's story without correcting or disputing it.

Similarly, when we tell the other person how we see things, we can help them make sense of *our* behavior. Starting with words like "from my perspective" increases the likelihood the other person will hear us. We are simply offering our point of view, not claiming the "truth."

THE CHARACTERS

Every story has characters. The more interesting the characters, the more compelling the story. The characters provide depth as we identify with their thoughts, feelings, hopes, and fears. As readers or listeners, our connection to and empathy with the characters draw us into the story.

Here's what might be going on inside the same disgruntled employee as a character in her own conflict story:

- She feels disrespected and excluded when she is not consulted on the changes
- She believes she was being helpful in pointing out the pitfalls of the changes
- She feels misunderstood and unfairly attacked
- She fears her manager will judge or even punish her for speaking up

From her words and actions, we might assume we know what she thinks and feels, but we won't know for sure unless she tells us. And she may not tell us unless she is asked to and feels she can do so without being further attacked or sinking deeper into the conflict.

Notice in her conflict story how quickly she moved around the drama triangle. Her perspective shifted from the role of hero (pointing out the pitfalls) to victim (feeling unfairly criticized) back to hero (seeking justice for the abusive treatment). As her temper got the better of her, she slipped into being the villain when she personally attacked her boss by calling him a "joke." Conversely, her boss likely experienced a similar trip around the drama triangle, seeing himself first as the hero (for trying to save the department through his changes) and then feeling victimized by the employee's lack of appreciation and subsequent personal attack.

Although the facts provide a starting point from which we can *identify* a conflict, insight into the characters allows us to *understand* the conflict. The thoughts, feelings, and motives of those involved in conflict help us make sense of their behavior. A co-worker withdraws, for example, and is unresponsive when we attempt to communicate. We label them as aloof or uncooperative. They see themselves as reacting to some earlier slight or as simply trying to cope with personal problems about which we have no knowledge.

When people are unable to resolve conflict, it seldom is because they lack the ability to problem solve. Two people who can define a problem and who agree to work together to solve it usually are successful. However, emotion and conflict are entwined. Unmanaged emotion, often anger, prevents us from reaching a common understanding of a problem and dampens any desire to work with the other person to solve it. Our mistrust leads us to see the other person as the problem (the villain).

We cannot fully understand a conflict until we understand the thoughts and feelings of those involved — the characters in our conflict stories. Yet experience has taught us that the frustration and anger that accompany conflict are at best uncomfortable and at worst dangerous. When we view the other person as the villain, we assume they intend to do us harm. It's not surprising then that we hesitate to emerge from behind our walls of judgment and defensiveness. We are reluctant to open what we fear to be a Pandora's box of emotion. This is where we need to draw on a different type of hero's courage, for until we are willing to take this risk, little will change. It would be like looking in the mirror and waiting for our reflection to move first.

We can start by clarifying our motives and letting the other person know our thoughts or feelings. This transparency may broaden their perspective and cause them to at least entertain the possibility that we aren't the villain they have made us out to be.

It is equally important to stay curious about the other character in our conflict story. What motivated them to behave as they did? What were they attempting to communicate or achieve? What were they thinking or feeling? By discovering this, we gain a deeper understanding of the conflict and are that much closer to resolving it. If we understand their motive or reasons, we may be able to release our judgment of *them* as the villain. Once this happens, we can begin to view each other as partners and work together to explore new ways to solve the problem.

THE THEME (CONFLICT AS UNMET NEEDS)

A theme is a recurring idea — the thread that weaves its way throughout a story and unifies it. Themes of novels, movies, or even newspaper articles involve conflict in some form. As the needs and values of the characters clash (within themselves, with each other, or with the world), conflict emerges. Stress and tension increase. We are drawn in. Ratings soar.

The American Heritage Dictionary of the English Language defines conflict as "opposition between characters or forces in a work of drama or fiction, especially opposition that motivates or shapes the action of the plot." This definition would include internal conflict — an individual torn between pacifism and revenge, for example.

Conflict provides a story with its juice. Without conflict, we would have no victims, villains, or heroes — no drama triangle. Stories without conflict lack the suspense and tension that captivate us. As screenwriters say, nothing moves without conflict. Our personal conflict stories would not hold our audiences (or rally support for our cause) without drama.

Because a good dramatic story attracts attention (often in the form of sympathy), some people seem to be addicted to conflict. You probably know people who are guaranteed to have conflict brewing somewhere at any given time. If things smooth out at work, something on the home front erupts. Even people who may avoid conflict like the plague often experience it vicariously by gossiping about other people's conflicts.

To understand someone's conflict story, uncover the theme. Ask yourself what might be the underlying and unmet need that fuels their conflict. Consider conflict as a quest to recover what was taken from us or to protect what is threatened. This understanding will lead us to frame the conflict in terms of interests and needs. It becomes a problem to solve rather than a battle to fight.

What drives us?

In the 1940s, psychologist Abraham Maslow suggested that human beings are driven by a set of needs, which he arranged in a hierarchy.

The most basic are those associated with survival (air, food, shelter), closely followed by the need for safety. When these needs are denied or threatened, physical confrontation and war may result. The more basic the need, the more primal the conflict.

FIGURE 3A
MASLOW'S HIERARCHY
OF NEEDS

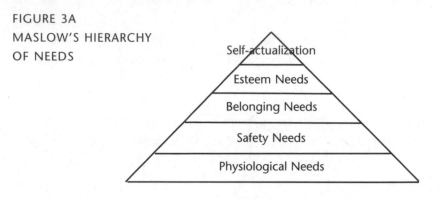

In our day-to-day lives in Western society, we are fortunate that survival and physical safety seldom fuel our conflicts. More often, we focus on belonging and esteem needs. Most conflict in families and organizations occurs at this level. If you listen to people complain about their workplace or family, you will hear much more about disrespectful treatment or lack of fairness than you will about money and safety. At the root of conflict lie unmet needs. Consciously or subconsciously, these needs drive us and motivate our behavior. And when we perceive that something or someone stands between us and fulfilling our needs, we cast them as the villain.

When our needs go unmet, our body lets us know, even though we often ignore its signals. If we are open to these signals, they can assist us to identify the unmet needs that lie at the root of our conflict. Think of times when you have felt your "button being pushed" and found yourself becoming angry. Your particular "button" links to an unmet need, and the resulting anger tells you that "what's happening here is unacceptable — something has got to change." If we can overcome our impulse to attack our perceived enemy, we can allow our anger to inform us about our needs and values.

INTERNAL CONFLICT

Sometimes our needs contradict each other and spark internal conflict: we may seek to belong, yet value our independence; we demand fairness and consistency, yet want to be treated as a unique individual. Let's revisit our employee's story for a minute. She felt victimized by her villainous manager, who, from her perspective, imposed unworkable changes without consultation and attacked her when she spoke up. She experienced the new manager as trampling her overall need for respect and, more specifically, her needs:

- to be included and consulted
- to be heard
- to feel competent in her job

Such unmet needs might fuel *internal conflict*. The employee might be torn between her need for financial security ("This is a good job. I'll just put up with this new guy and wait out these changes") and her need for respect ("I won't take this lying down"). She also might be torn between her urge to confront the manager ("Don't ever do that to me again!") and her need for safety ("He'll really make life tough for me if I say anything more").

This inner conflict is not necessarily negative — we can think of it as simply energy. Anger and frustration can be powerful catalysts for change and can spur us to act. The employee can choose how to channel that energy. Does she stew and simmer in frustration? Does she explore other jobs where she would be more included or respected? Or does the inner conflict propel her to gather her courage and approach her manager directly to express her concerns and attempt to resolve the situation? The choice she makes speaks volumes about her values and priorities.

INTERPERSONAL CONFLICT

Often our unmet needs involve other people and lead to interpersonal conflict. The employee's interpersonal conflict with her manager could surface in the form of a grievance or an argument over a particular policy. The conflict might go underground and involve gossip, passive resistance, and passive-aggressive behavior (I hope she doesn't make his coffee in the morning). Regardless, there would be an undercurrent of tension whenever the two were together.

Such interpersonal conflict also can be traced to unmet needs. The employee feels neither respected nor supported by the manager and accordingly sees him as the villain. Yet the manager strives to meet his own needs. He, too, wants to be seen as competent and to be respected in the organization. He might even share the employee's need for financial security and fear the loss of his job. He may not even be aware of the unmet needs that drive him — but may feel threatened by the employee and make her the villain in his story.

So rather than casting people as villains in our conflicts, let's remember that both we and our apparent adversary are driven by the same basic human needs that Maslow identified more than 50 years ago. Our unmet needs often are shrouded by anger and encased in fear. As listeners, our challenge is to withstand the heat of these emotions and hear another person's entire story. Conversely, as speakers, we must tell our story and express our needs in a way that doesn't paint the other person as the villain.

Our conflict dramas

We make sense of our conflicts through story and it shouldn't come as a surprise that our stories and the dramas of stage and screen follow similar patterns. The victims, villains, and heroes of our interpersonal conflicts mirror those portrayed in movies (minus the odd photon torpedo or wizard's spell). As you read the standard movie plot line that follows, see how it might fit with a conflict in your life.

When we watch a movie, we begin by experiencing the status quo world of the main character. Writers often refer to this as *the platform*. In *The Wizard of Oz*, we meet Dorothy as she innocently goes about her business in rural Kansas. In interpersonal conflict, there is always a "before." "Things were fine before they made George a supervisor; now he acts like Attila the Hun" or "We got along fine before they brought in that new software."

Once the platform is established, we encounter the *inciting incident* — something "tilts the platform" and creates conflict. The main character may be in conflict with another person, with themselves, or with their world. The tornado in "The Wizard of Oz" would be the inciting incident that tilted Dorothy's platform. In interpersonal conflict, the inciting incident occurs the moment we see ourselves as attacked or threatened — when we first felt "hit." In some cases this may be a minor incident that serves as the proverbial straw that broke the camel's back.

The inciting incident leads to *struggle and conflict*. The victim often adopts the mantle of hero in an attempt to right the wrong or recover what has been lost. As the hero overcomes one obstacle, another often surfaces, and all may appear lost — the darkness before the dawn. Dorothy's journey and discovery that the wizard was a sham would mark this part of the story. Interpersonal conflict likewise can be considered a quest to recover what has been lost or protect what is threatened. At some point in the quest, the hero feels overwhelmed, trapped, and tempted to abandon the journey. Many people in conflict reach this point.

Then comes the *turning point*. Something shifts within the protagonist. Perhaps they begin to believe in themselves, forgive someone, or take the risk they thought themselves unable to take. Dorothy, in confronting the Wicked Witch of the West and defending Toto, discovers her previously untapped power. In interpersonal conflict, the turning point could be a shift from judgment to curiosity, a point when we let go of the need to be right or punish and instead seek to understand and collaborate.

Finally, we reach the story's *climax* as the rejuvenated hero confronts (and usually overcomes) the final obstacle — the villain. The climax leads to *resolution*. Dorothy vanquishes the Wicked Witch of the West and discovers the path home. In our interpersonal conflicts, we vanquish the problem by creating a solution that works for all involved.

And to complete the story, we *return to the platform* as we see how events have impacted the characters and their world. The platform is again in equilibrium, though a new equilibrium. Dorothy returns to Kansas, a changed person in a familiar world. In conflict, this change is reflected in the deepened relationship and improved trust that often emerge when we are able to collaboratively resolve an issue.

When I first heard this typical plot line described at a workshop, I was stunned by its similarity to conflicts I had mediated. People in conflict often feel hopelessly stuck — trapped in *struggle*. My involvement as a mediator often was seen as a last resort, yet often became a *turning point*. I did not fix the problem for them but helped them view each other and the problem differently. This shift in attitude and approach allowed people to move from struggle to resolution.

The other parallel I saw between the standard plot line and conflict was the growth of the protagonist as a result of the journey. To overcome the obstacles they face, they may have to draw on an inner strength or change their approach. Conflict similarly provides an opportunity for us to learn about ourselves, clarify our values, and broaden our perspectives.

When did the knife go in?

To get to the heart of a conflict, identify its inciting incident, the moment in the story when "the knife went in." The metaphor of the knife going in helps us identify the moment when someone experienced being victimized and began to see the other person as the villain. Other metaphors for this concept would include an electric shock, a punch to the stomach, a cut, a slamming door, or a rug being pulled out from under. All describe the moment they first felt "hit."

Apply this metaphor to a conflict in your own life. Think of a time you felt angry or resentful toward another, then examine events and ask yourself when exactly you first felt "hit." When did you begin to see the other person as the enemy? What triggered you? What was your unmet need?

Although conflict resolution focuses on the future, we cannot ignore these past wounds. Everyone involved needs an opportunity to express their hurt, anger, or disappointment. Until they feel acknowledged, they are unlikely to relinquish their role as victim and will continue to view the other person as a villain. This belief traps them on the drama triangle and prevents resolution. It also explains why conflict sometimes surfaces over petty matters. Those involved usually have seen each other as villains for so long they simply pick a convenient issue over which to continue their battle. The issue is an opportunity to reinforce their ingrained judgment of the other person as untrustworthy, uncaring, etc.

Because there are two sides to every conflict, it helps us to learn when the other person felt "the knife go in." When did they feel "hit?" When did their defenses go up? This point of wounding provides us with a starting point to explore how the conflict has impacted the other person. By asking them and listening to their answer without judging, we build empathy and encourage our adversary to join us in moving beyond the drama triangle toward resolution.

The journey from confrontation to collaboration

Conflict can be seen as a quest. In myths and movies, heroes use their wits and courage to surmount the obstacles they encounter on their quest. When all seems lost, they may rely on knowledge or a gift they received along the way. Subsequent chapters of this book will identify some of the barriers we face on the journey through conflict toward resolution and provide tools to overcome those barriers. (You'll need to provide your own wits and courage.)

Through real-life scenarios played out by the employees of Turm-Oil Inc., we will explore ways to move beyond the drama triangle. Though the characters are fictional, you may find the situations they face all too familiar. Join this dysfunctional work "family" as they develop new perspectives and new approaches to conflict on their journey from confrontation to collaboration.

Summary

Remember that the full story includes the plot, the characters, and the theme. Although the events of the story provide a starting point from which we can *identify* a conflict, insight into the characters allows us to *understand* the conflict. Finally, the theme involves the needs that drive us and motivate our behavior.

Unmet needs might fuel internal conflict or interpersonal conflict.

To get to the heart of a conflict, identify its inciting incident (the moment in the story when "the knife went in") and explore the needs that have been threatened or denied as a result of that event.

From theory to practice

Analyse a conflict in which you were or are involved:
- When did the knife go in for me?
- What need was wounded or threatened?
- When might the knife have gone in for the other person?
- What need of theirs might have been wounded or threatened?

CHAPTER 4

WELCOME TO TURM-OIL INC.

Lubricating the flaxseed community for over 20 years

Co-workers in conflict

Welcome to Turm-Oil Inc., a major distributor of flaxseed oil. In this fictitious yet typical workplace, employees consider themselves to be family — one large, dysfunctional family. Though many of you may see yourselves in the cast, I can assure you that these characters are composites of personalities, styles, and qualities of hundreds of people and organizations I have worked with (except Gale, and she knows who she is). Some live to work, others work to live; but whatever their reasons, they spend more time with each other than with their families.

As a company, Turm-Oil Inc. is facing the typical challenges of the new millennium: downsizing, greater reliance on technology, increased competition, and demanding customers. Such changes lead inevitably to conflict and produce no shortage of drama. Now meet our players (in order of appearance):

Clyde S. Dale

Clyde S. Dale, General Manager: He is an old dog, and these are very new tricks.

Clyde's haggard face reflects 25 years surviving in the dog-eat-dog business world. Clyde is well-intentioned, though hard-pressed to keep up with the changing face of the work-place. He has paid his dues by swallowing his pride and following orders and can't understand why others don't do the same. His intense focus on operational concerns and concrete results doesn't leave much time or energy for what he sees as the petty, touchy-feely stuff. He ignores problems until they boil over, at which time he takes charge and straightens things out. Fearing that being seen as "wrong" will undermine his respect, he covers his basic good-heart-ed nature with a gruffness that leads others to experience him as blunt and uncaring.

Vic Tom, Salesman: The customers are easy to deal with; it's his co-workers who are the problem.

Hired four years ago to buoy sagging sales, Vic has produced sporadic results. He can be personable and has built solid relationships with Turm-Oil's major customers. Unfortunately, he shows little regard for "those office types," whom he views as a necessary evil. He is frustrated by policies and procedures and regularly reminds staff that the customers (and sales) are number one. Though he seems to be always on the run, he's never too busy to tell you how busy he is. Away from the office, he usually can be found on the golf course (or "networking," as he prefers to call it).

Vic Tom

Perry Noyd, Controller: Maybe the sky *is* falling — and you heard it from him first.

Perry has seen it all in his 22 years with Turm-Oil and has the scars to prove it. He knows that unless he attends to every last detail, things will fall between the cracks and he'll be the scapegoat. Those without his appreciation for precision experience him as anal-retentive. Life has taught him that nothing is as good

Perry Noyd

as it appears, and he often raises the "devil's advocate" point of view during meetings. He sees himself as a realist and can't fathom why others characterize him as negative — or why he ends up eating lunch alone so often. Through it all, his passion for gardening has persisted (including his obsession with weeds and aphids).

Doug Right, Manager of Distribution: The company would run so much better if people would only do things *his* way.

This strapping 44-year-old was brought into the company two years ago to shape up the disaster area that was distribution. He has strong ideas about the way things should be and isn't shy in voicing them or initiating change. He has produced excellent results through his energy and commitment, yet remains puzzled why his team fails to share his enthusiasm and seems to need constant direction. He works on curbing his volatile temper and sees it as progress that as coach for his son's Little League team he was suspended only once last season.

Doug Right

Dean Isle, Systems Technician: The more he has to deal with people, the more he likes his computer.

In his mid-20s and relatively new to the company, Dean is extremely capable and comfortable with technology. It's people who cause him the real problems. When things get hot, he retreats to the sanctum of his back office and the comforts of e-mail. Shy by nature, he seldom lets down his guard and is seen by some as aloof and unfriendly. He is so uncomfortable with conflict that he clings to his belief that "if you leave it alone long enough, it will go away." He often is heard commenting, "It's not that big a deal," though rumor has it he vents his frustrations by playing Doom online when he goes home.

Dean Isle

Dinah Myte

Dinah Myte, Office Manager: As long as people realize this is *her* office, there shouldn't be any problems.

While working her way up in the company over the past 18 years, Dinah has learned to stand up for herself. Extremely capable and hardworking, she has an attention to detail that leads her to live by the letter of the law and causes frequent flare-ups with customers and co-workers. She sees the world in black and white and has little patience for those who may see shades of gray. She's here to do the job — and do it right. Her outspokenness and adherence to policy inspire fear in many who approach her.

Melanie "Mel" Low, Receptionist: She tries to keep everyone happy, but conflict finds her nonetheless.

In her early 20s and new to business, Melanie sees the world through "new age" eyes. She believes everyone should get along and is the one who organizes social events and bakes the birthday cakes. She always looks for ways to improve the workplace, which frustrates Clyde, who views her suggestions as a distraction from the task at hand. She is quick to empathize with others and usually sees both points of view in any situation. Because she values harmony, she is reluctant to assert herself for fear of rocking the boat. When resentment builds, she tends to withdraw and suffer in silence, but when she reaches her limit, look out!

Melanie Low

Lance A. Lott, Warehouseman and Staff Representative: Wherever management threatens, he will be there.

For ten of his 14 years with the company, Lance has stood up for his fellow workers as staff rep. Caring and passionate about people's right to fair treatment, he is quick to react when injustice rears its ugly head. Privately, he admits to enjoying the odd moment of righteous indignation. Time has taught him to be

Lance Lott

suspicious of management motives, yet he's seen enough over the years to realize there are two sides to every story. He often feels he's fighting the good fight "against all odds," but he perseveres. After a tumultuous start, he and Gale have forged a solid working relationship based on their shared practicality and grudging respect for each other's candor.

Gale Reasoner, Human Resources Consultant: Even though she understands people, they still drive her crazy.

With more than 20 years in human resources, Gale recently "retired" from Turm-Oil and now consults from her home office. This change allows her to maintain a healthy distance from bureaucracy and office politics, for which she has little patience. She believes in collaboration and has the knowledge and skills this requires. She must work hard, however, to curb her basic feisty nature and to take the time and energy to remain curious. She and Clyde have been known to butt heads, but she is one of the few people able to engage him productively. Her effectiveness in doing so has caused Clyde to say, "I'm glad you're on our side." Very sociable and fun-loving, she is prone to the occasional guffaw or snappy retort (not always at the appropriate time).

Gale Reasoner

Marko Blunt, Shipper: There is never a question about where he stands, though sometimes it's on people's toes.

Nearing retirement after 15 years with Turm-Oil, this stocky 58-year-old tells it like it is. He occasionally rubs people the wrong way with his excitability and bluntness, though his energy and humor endear him to most. He is more prone to talk than to listen, as reflected in his trademark, finger-wagging "Just hold on one minute there." His mistrust of authority and of "the suits" is well known in the office.

Marko Blunt

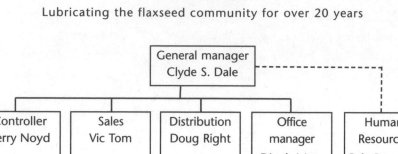

TURM-OIL INC.

Lubricating the flaxseed community for over 20 years

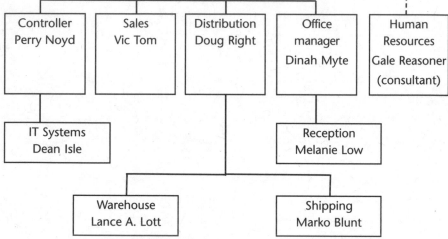

Who's who at Turm-Oil Inc.

Black Friday

As a result of a sluggish economy, spiraling expenses, and a negative product review by the prestigious Health Oil Monthly, Turm-Oil Inc. suffered its worst quarter in history. This prompted general manager Clyde Dale to make some drastic changes. The resulting stress awakened slumbering resentments among our happy family, as the minutes of the quarterly management meeting will attest.

MINUTES OF THE QUARTERLY MANAGEMENT MEETING

Location: Boardroom at Turm-Oil Inc.
Minutes by Melanie Low
Present:
Clyde Dale, General Manager
Perry Noyd, Controller

Dinah Myte, Office Manager
Doug Right, Distribution
Vic Tom, Sales
Dean Isle, IT Systems
Regrets: Gale Reasoner, HR Consultant

Clyde reviewed the quarterly sales figures and expressed concern over a decline from the previous quarter. Vic provided his report for the quarter and explained reasons for the decline. Spirited discussion ensued. No decision was reached.

Clyde advised that because of the decline in revenue, the sales office will be closed. Vic therefore will require office space. The group debated where to locate Vic but despite spirited discussion was unable to agree. Clyde then determined that Vic would take over the boardroom as his office.

Doug advised that he will be meeting with Dean to discuss concerns with the new inventory control software.

Clyde asked if there were any other issues. None was raised.

Meeting was adjourned.

What the fly on the wall heard

The minutes fail to capture what really occurred in the Turm-Oil boardroom.

Clyde Dale frowns as he strides into the boardroom and surveys his assembled team. "Let's get on with this," he growls and draws a spreadsheet from his briefcase. "I won't beat around the bush. The numbers for the first quarter stink. We're hurting and, frankly, if you don't turn things around, there'll be some changes around here."

He pauses and scans the table, but only receptionist Melanie Low meets his eyes. "What do you mean?" she asks innocently.

Clyde wastes no time responding to the invitation. His jaw tightens and his voice strains. "Where do you want me to start? How about sales?" He glares at sales manager Vic Tom, who leans forward ever so slightly. "Sales are down 22 percent and there's not much more to say about that other than that they better pick up."

This seems to be the opening Vic has been waiting for. He draws himself up, then very deliberately begins his defense. "I've been knocking myself out for this company. There's no way you can blame me for this. If I got the support I've been asking for, sales wouldn't be a problem."

At the far corner of the table, office manager Dinah Myte and controller Perry Noyd glance at each other. Dinah's rolling eyes meet Perry's humorless smile and disbelieving shake of his head. Vic's eyes land on Perry. "I told you from the get-go that I needed more face-to-face contact with our customers. What do you do? Cut my travel budget. We were the only major flax-oil distributor not to attend the Wellness Show last month. You bean counters are making us look second-rate."

Perry's response appears to be well-rehearsed. "Don't even think of blaming your sales numbers on not being able to attend the Wellness Show. You didn't even go last year and you always complain it's a waste of time. Besides, Vic, you're not the only one in this office with budget demands. I'm not Santa Claus, you know. There's only so much to go around."

"Well, no sales, no company. So of course sales are important, even if no one around here seems to think so. Plus I can't sell what we don't have in stock." At this he turns his attention to distribution manager Doug Right. "I keep telling you people that customers won't wait. They all need it yesterday." Gathering steam, he continues, "And another thing, I spend half my time in the field putting out fires because you guys in the warehouse screw up every second order. When am I going to get some support around here?"

Doug flips his pencil in the air. "You'll get some as soon as we get some. I've told Dean a dozen times that the inventory software needs to be upgraded. All I get is him telling me these things are complicated." Doug waves the back of his hand dismissively in system technician Dean Isle's direction. "You haven't heard the last from me on this, Dean."

Eyes shift toward Dean, who seems preoccupied with his Palm Pilot. He looks up, startled, then freezes — the proverbial deer caught in the headlights of conflict. He clears his throat as his eyes dart between Doug and Vic. "I'm working on the system. These things are complicated. Look, send me an e-mail with details of the problem and I'll call the software provider again." His voice trails off into a mumble.

Vic shakes his head in disbelief. His jaw tenses. His widening eyes land on Dinah. He sputters, "You people can't even get me brochures for the annual trade show."

Dinah is having none of this. As soon as she hears "brochures," she's off and running, talking over the irate Vic. "I told you three times how much lead time the printer needed, but you were just tooooo busy and important to bother with details like that. Don't you dare blame me for your stupidity."

Vic's face reddens and his voice rises as he leaps from his seat and slams his palm down on the table. "My stupidity?! You're all so busy covering your own butts you haven't heard anything I've said. This is … oh, forget it!" With this, Vic snaps his briefcase shut, shoves his chair backward, and storms from the room sputtering to himself.

Those who remain fidget in an awkward hush. Clyde grinds his jaw in exasperation. Melanie finally breaks the silence. "Anyone for a muffin?"

When the meeting resumes 15 minutes later, Clyde ploughs forward. "I'll get Vic straightened out later. Right now we have to find a place for him in the office. I've had to close our other office with the drop in sales."

"What?" a startled Dinah blurts. "You saw what he just did to me. And now you want me to welcome him? Good luck!"

Clyde takes a deep breath, fighting the urge to explode. "Just calm down, Dinah, and talk about this rationally."

"Calm down?! You calm down! You're not the one he's harassing."

"Okay, okay," says Clyde. "You're right. Maybe he was out of line, but he still needs a place to work."

"Well, there's just no room for him. We're jammed as it is."

"Look, that may be true, but you're going to have to find a way to fit him in."

Dinah seems to reluctantly accept that Vic will be somewhere on the premises. She sighs and shrugs. "Let's just put him next to Melanie. There's some room up there."

Melanie looks up and arches her eyebrows. "No, there's not! Besides, it's already too noisy at the front with everyone hanging around the coffee machine and traipsing into the boardroom. I don't have anything against Vic personally ..." She pauses and chooses her words carefully, then continues in a breathless rush, "But he's so loud, I just couldn't concentrate."

Turm-Oil in action

Dinah is not ready to have the problem pushed back at her so quickly. "I don't know what the big deal is, Melanie. Not much happens out there anyway. You should be able to handle it."

This is too much for even the mild-mannered Melanie. "Not much happens?! A lot happens out there. You just don't see it because you're stuck in your office with those papers. All you have to do is move some of your stuff from the photocopy area and Vic could use that space."

"And where would we put the photocopier and the files? I'm not walking all the way to the warehouse every time I need something."

Doug now jumps in. "Slow down a minute. What's this about the warehouse? We already have enough of other people's junk back there. And then people have the gall to tell me to keep the warehouse tidier because customers come back there to see the samples. No way anything else is going back there."

Dinah turns to Clyde. "So there you go. There's no room at the inn. Let him fend for himself until he learns some manners."

She no sooner concludes her pronouncement than the door opens and a subdued Vic, eyes downcast, re-enters the room and quietly returns to his seat.

Clyde is near the end of his rope on this issue. "I can't believe it. We're facing our worst quarter ever and this group can't even work out something this simple. Okay, then, I'll decide. Vic will use the boardroom. Case closed."

Looks of alarm precede a flurry of objections, and Clyde's decree even brings the daydreaming Dean back to reality. "Where will we eat lunch? It's bad enough Vic gets to 'network' on the company tab for lunch while we brown bag it. I'm already stuck in that broom closet at the back. Now you want me to eat lunch there too?"

Perry slowly stands, drawing on his 22 years as the company's financial conscience. "What about our meetings? We earmarked this space for meetings when we moved into this office. I warned everyone way back then that someone would want to grab it for an office, but people said we wouldn't let that happen. And here we are doing it?"

Clyde is unmoved. "I said, case closed. You had your chance to work it out among yourselves and didn't, so don't blame me. This meeting is adjourned." With that, Clyde makes straight for his office, where a slamming door reflects his frustration.

Dinah gathers her notes and glares once more at Melanie. "Way to go, Melanie. You cost us our meeting room," she hisses before striding from the room. Melanie can think of nothing better than to stick out her tongue at the back of the departing Dinah's head.

In the chapters to come we will follow our cast and see how they fare as they apply new approaches and new tools to resolve these thorny issues.

CHAPTER 5

THE ASSUMPTION ICEBERG

If I feel like a victim, you must be the villain.

Assumptions weave their way throughout conflict. You may say or do something that triggers me. I feel threatened, excluded, or disrespected and see myself as a victim. To play that role, I require a villain. You, of course, are the likely candidate and I therefore attribute malicious motives to your words and actions. If I feel hurt, you must have intended to hurt me. I judge you as uncaring, inconsiderate, and controlling — unmistakably a villain. You, meanwhile, have your own perspective on these same events. You know your motives to be pure. You become the misunderstood hero — a well-intentioned victim of my unfair judgments. Here we have two very different perspectives on the same event. And seldom the twain shall meet.

Let's look at a situation in which assumptions led to a conflict at Turm-Oil Inc. a few months before Black Friday.

Book 'em, Dinah
DINAH'S STORY

The warehouse door slams behind her as Dinah Myte weaves her way among the strewn pallets of flaxseed oil to Lance Lott's workstation. Her frown announces that this will not be a social visit. She plunks herself in a chair.

"Clyde's gone too far this time. This is the last straw."

Lance leans forward in anticipation. "What did he do this time?"

"This is the last straw."

"He put Melanie in charge of booking the boardroom. I've spent hours creating a system that finally works and he takes the bookings away from me. And he didn't even have the decency to tell me to my face. I was straightening Dean out for not booking the room he was using when he told me he *did* book the room — through Melanie. That little weasel Dean looked so smug I wanted to wring his neck."

"Okay. Forget Dean for now. It's Clyde who's the problem. He has no right to change your job out of the blue. I can't believe that guy."

"Not only didn't he ask me about it, he didn't even have the nerve to *tell* me about it. I was the last to know and ended up looking like a fool in front of Dean, of all people."

"We have enough to do to keep this place running without Clyde pulling this sort of garbage. We need to do something," says Lance.

"I think he's trying to get back at me for the last staff meeting," replies Dinah glumly.

"Yeah?"

"Well, you know Clyde and his new 'teamwork' approach. He always tells us to 'talk about our issues.' So when he asked how things were going, I told him that we need another person to help us keep up with all the paperwork from this new system. He gave me that phony 'I hear you' look and then walked out. The next thing I know, he's taken away one of the few things I enjoy about my job. It's a slap in the face."

"That's just outrageous."

"He also doesn't realize that there's more to booking rooms than just typing in the appointments. That prima donna Vic has to have things just so — this type of setup, that type of muffins. And you know I'll be the

"Dinah should be happy I got her some help."

one taking the flak if it's not done right."

"What a bunch."

"So you think I have a case? I hope so, because I'm not taking this lying down!"

Lance narrows his eyes, picks up the phone, and punches in Clyde's extension.

CLYDE'S STORY

A few minutes later, Clyde plops himself down across the board-room table from Gale Reasoner. He stares into space and shakes his head ruefully. He takes a deep breath. "There is no pleasing some people. I don't even know why I try. I bend over backward to help and all I get is a kick in the teeth."

"Ouch. Sounds like you had another visit from Lance."

"Well, not yet, but he just went ballistic on the phone. Some story about undermining staff. Dinah whines about too much work, I lighten her load, and now I'm the bad guy! You can't win with some people."

"Ah, the joy of managing — you're between a rock and a hard place."

"You got that right. So what am I going to do about this? Lance sounds like he's ready for battle."

"What's this about?"

"He said something about Dinah being undermined because I told people to book the boardroom through Melanie. I figured that would take some of the load off Dinah. She somehow came up with the hare-brained idea that I did it to punish her for something. Who can figure?"

"I lighten her load and now I'm the bad guy!"

"So you were trying to help her out, but she thought you were trying to show her up. You assumed she'd appreciate the change, but instead she went through the roof."

Clyde contemplates Gale's pithy summary, considers restating his innocence, but thinks better of it. Finally he concedes, "That's it in a nutshell. So what do I do now?"

"You'd better figure out where this went off the rails. It seems to be me you both made some assumptions, but neither one of you checked them out."

"You can't tell me she didn't know that I was trying to help her out. She's just a troublemaker, plain and simple. She'll do anything to make me look like the bad guy."

"Perhaps, but what do you think set her off?"

"How should I know?"

"You might ask her."

Clyde looks as though he's just bitten into a lemon. "So you think I should make sure she knows that I was trying to help?"

"Well, that and find out why she's ticked off."

"Look, I'll talk to her but I'm not apologizing for trying to help her out."

Gale can't resist a gentle jibe as Clyde gets up to leave. "Good luck — and remember to breathe."

Motive and impact

In conflict, we judge our own actions by our motives. We judge others' actions by the impact they have on us.

To understand how widely divergent perspectives (stories) can coexist, examine the difference between the *motive* behind someone's words and actions and the *impact* of those words and actions. *Our* motives, we like to think, are always noble, even heroic. Yet when *others* say or do something, we experience the impact — and, in conflict, feel victimized.

In Dinah's story, she

- knows Clyde reassigned boardroom bookings without consulting her (the events)
- feels victimized (disrespected and embarrassed) because Clyde neither consulted her on his decision nor communicated the change to her directly (the impact of the events)
- sees herself as the hero when she stands up to Clyde by involving Lance to ensure she receives fair treatment (her motive)

Based on how she was impacted, Dinah assumes:

- that Clyde intended to embarrass her (and is the villain)
- that he should know she was simply acting in self-defense when she complained to Lance (that Clyde understood her motive)

The diagram below helps explain how two people can view a situation so differently. Think of the *events* as the tip of an iceberg, visible to both people. Thoughts and feelings (*motive* and *impact*) lie beneath the surface. We know our own, but can only guess the other person's. We assume we know what the other person was thinking or feeling and weave those assumptions into our stories. We treat our assumptions as "truth," though we see only part of the picture.

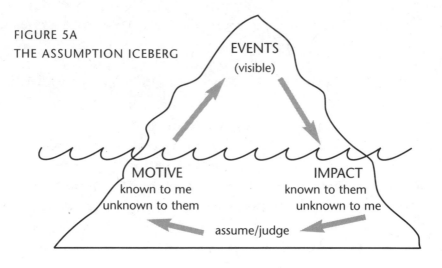

FIGURE 5A
THE ASSUMPTION ICEBERG

EVENTS
(visible)

MOTIVE
known to me
unknown to them

IMPACT
known to them
unknown to me

assume/judge

MAKING ASSUMPTIONS

Dinah and Clyde's situation serves as an example of how assumptions shape conflict stories. Dinah's and Clyde's stories would include similar events:

- Clyde asked Melanie to handle booking the boardroom
- Clyde didn't speak with Dinah first
- Dinah asked Lance to intervene

Both motive and impact, however, remain unclear, distorted by the murky waters of assumption, judgment, and anger. Clyde and Dinah are both trapped on the drama triangle — each feels "hit" first (and misunderstood) and sees the other person as the villain. Each knows his or her side of the story; neither understands the full story. This is another example of a conflict story where knowing the characters, their feelings, and their motives is vital to resolution.

Clarifying assumptions

This situation might change if either person started to shift from judgment to curiosity. Clyde might approach Dinah and ask how she saw things and how she felt when she heard about the change in responsibilities. Likewise, Dinah could ask Clyde what he was intending to achieve and what his reasoning was for not discussing his decision with her first.

Alternatively, either could share their perspective so more of the "iceberg" becomes visible. Clyde could let Dinah know that he was attempting to respond to her concerns and that he felt shocked when she went to Lance instead of talking to him directly. Dinah could tell Clyde how she felt on hearing about the change from Dean. Such communication "surfaces" the conflict and allows each person to see the bigger picture (see diagram below). Once they identify the problem, they can "separate the people from the problem." They can redirect their emotional energy from fuming about the other person to solving the problem and improving the situation.

FIGURE 5B: SURFACING MOTIVE AND IMPACT

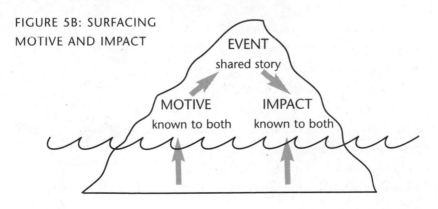

Book 'em, Dinah (revisited)

Either Clyde or Dinah could make the first move to clarify the situation, but let's see what happens when Clyde takes the initiative (he is the manager, after all) and approaches Dinah a few days later.

"Ten minutes, please, Dinah?" Clyde asks stiffly.

Dinah stops wrestling with her spreadsheet and warily eyes her boss. "Shields up, Mr. Worf," she thinks to herself as she offers a grudging "I guess."

They slip into the empty boardroom.

"You've been staring daggers at me all week," Clyde blurts. "What's your problem?"

"You pulling the rug out from under me is my problem," Dinah shoots back.

"What on earth are you talking about?"

"You took boardroom bookings away from me — just because I spoke up at the last staff meeting. How can you expect me to manage this office when the receptionist knows more than I do?!"

"You pulling the rug out from under me is my problem."

Clyde appears taken aback; his furrowed brow hints that the wheels are turning. "Wait a minute. I wasn't trying to get back at you. I was trying to help you."

"You sure have a funny way of helping — leaving me in the dark like that."

"Hold it. First you ask for extra help, then you make me the bad guy when I get some for you." Clyde looks to the heavens with arms spread wide and sighs. "At the last two staff meetings you said we couldn't take on anything new until we got on top of our paperwork. I wanted to free up some of your time by getting Melanie to handle bookings for the boardroom. Besides, you're always complaining about Vic and his last-minute, urgent sales meetings."

Dinah looks a bit surprised and begins to entertain the unlikely notion that Clyde

"I was trying to help you."

might actually have listened to her. "Vic *is* a pain. He thinks the world revolves around him and he'll push little Melanie around like a shopping cart if we let him. Next thing you know, we won't even be able to use our own boardroom."

"I'm lost — do you want some extra help or not?"

"Of course, but what I need most is some quiet time each morning. Just give me an hour without that stupid phone ringing and I'll be caught up in a week. We can't get anything done in the mornings with all the calls."

"Sure." Clyde's shoulders relax. His face shows a blend of surprise and relief. "Let me check it out with Melanie and get back to you by noon."

Dinah begins to entertain the unlikely notion that Clyde might actually have listened to her.

"Look, Clyde. I appreciate the help, I really do, but next time at least talk to me before changing things around, okay?" Dinah implores.

"Okay, okay," Clyde assures her, looking relieved to end the conversation.

With her dignity intact and all well in her kingdom, Dinah returns to her office with a small smile.

By staying curious, Clyde allowed Dinah to tell her story. He discovered she was ticked off primarily about being left out of the loop. He also learned she took pride in her ability to handle the demands of the bookings.

Once Dinah had a chance to tell her story, she was willing to listen to Clyde's reasons for what he did. She didn't agree with his actions but was able to gradually release her view of him as a villain and refocus on the problem at hand. Though their discussion was blunt, they managed to talk things out and open themselves to a broader perspective. This perspective allowed them to come up with a better solution and reduce the tension between them.

Summary

In conflict, we judge our own actions by our motives. We judge others' actions by the impact they have on us.

Think of the *events* as the tip of an iceberg, visible to both people. Thoughts and feelings (*motive* and *impact*) lie beneath the surface. We can reduce tension and clarify assumptions in two ways:

- Ask the other person what they intended by what they did or said; tell them the thinking behind our action
- Tell the other person how events impacted us; ask them how they were impacted by events

From theory to practice

Consider a conflict in your life and ask yourself the following questions:

- What assumptions am I making about the other person and their motives?
- How could I check out those assumptions?
- What assumptions might the other person be making about me and my motives? Why might they be seeing me as the villain?
- How might I clarify my motives and intention?

CHAPTER 6

THE WOBBLY STOOL OF CONFLICT

Ain't no use hurryin' if you're on the wrong road.
— Satchel Paige, ageless baseball pitcher

I often see people in conflict deadlocked over what appear to be minor issues. The harder they push their point of view, the tighter the other person clings to their own position. What prevents these intelligent, creative, and resourceful people from solving a simple problem? Their difficulty lies not in the size or complexity of the problem but in the way they approach each other and in rising emotions. They are "hurryin' " to resolve the conflict but failing to build the relationship necessary for collaboration.

As a kid, I saw that conflicts were settled in one of two ways. Certain issues were not open for negotiation. Those with the power decided how it would be: parents made rules, bigger kids commandeered the baseball diamond, and might made right. Those with less power seldom found it worthwhile to endure the pain that came with "negotiation." Other disagreements, however, could be settled by proving who was right. These arguments would be settled by reference to a dictionary, an encyclopedia, or *Goren's Bridge Complete*. Things were black or white, right or wrong, and I quickly learned the value of convincing the other person of the accuracy of my information and the rationale supporting my position. In hindsight, it is no surprise that I was attracted to the field of law, with its emphasis on facts, precedent, and logic.

As I got older, however, I found that my ability to prove my point seldom helped resolve my conflicts. My information and arguments were impeccable, my logic unimpeachable. I couldn't understand why my adversary remained unswayed and clung even more stubbornly to their views. The stress and tension that accompanied these deadlocks were both uncomfortable and mystifying. Clearly there were aspects to these conflicts of which I was unaware.

This pattern continued as I entered the workforce. Some people and I seemed able to solve any problem. We were a team, able to make the best of even the worst situation. Yet, with other people, the smallest issue could ignite a conflict that would quickly grow out of proportion. Over time, I realized that conflict resolution was more about relationship building than about problem-solving ability.

The three legs of conflict

People often tell me they feel lost and unsure in conflict. They can sense tension and defensiveness, yet are unable to pinpoint or address the cause.

This sense of wobbliness is like sitting on a three-legged stool with a loose leg. Each leg represents one aspect of a conflict: the *problem,* the *process,* and the *emotion.* If any one of these elements has not been addressed, our chances of effectively resolving an issue are slim. This comparison has served me personally and in my work as a mediator by providing a way to identify and address the resistance that may prevent resolution.

Most people are more comfortable dealing with the facts of a conflict than with the emotional element. Our impulse is to identify and solve the problem as quickly as possible. In our haste, however, we seldom take time to examine *how* we are approaching the problem and often minimize the impact of emotion. Try to identify the three legs of problem, process, and emotion in the following example from Turm-Oil Inc. Where do you think the resistance lies?

Big Bob goes bananas

The front door of the office has barely shut behind Gale Reasoner when Doug Right strides toward her. "You're finally here," he blurts out. Gale starts to respond, but Doug continues, "We've got big trouble with Marko. He's gone way over the line. He's got to go."

Gale enters the boardroom, slips off her coat, and exhales. "And good morning to you, Doug." Undaunted, he presses on. "Yeah, right. Good morning. Tell me what I have to do to get rid of Marko before he brings me and the company down."

"You know the rule, Doug. No crises before my first cup of coffee in the morning." Gale empties her briefcase and invites Doug to take a seat while she pours herself a cup of black coffee from the ever-present pot outside the boardroom. "Okay, Doug. Big trouble. You're ticked at Marko. What happened? From the beginning."

Convinced that someone is starting to understand his plight, Doug pauses long enough to take what seems like his first breath in the conversation, then plows ahead. "The beginning? First he screws up the Big Bob's Health Emporium order, then he stabs me in the back. What more is there to know?"

"I heard about a mix-up with Big Bob's. What happened?"

"Marko messed up the order — he forgot to include a flat of our new Certified Organic Banana Blend oil. Then when Big Bob phoned to complain, Marko got him even more upset and they ended up yelling at each other. Big Bob calls me and takes a strip off my hide. Said that two of their people double-checked the order and it was short. Then he complained that Marko yelled at him. Big Bob's a royal pain, but he's still one of our biggest customers. He's even threatening to pull their standing order."

"What did you do?"

"What could I do? I told Marko to personally take the missing flat over to Big Bob's and apologize for the whole fiasco. I had to eat crow with Bob, and you can imagine how much fun *that*

"Big Bob calls me and takes a strip off my hide."

was for me. Then I changed the procedure to make sure something like this would never happen again."

"So what's the problem? We can't fire Marko just because he made a mistake on one order. We both know he's a little hotheaded at times, but he usually calms down. Besides, he's been here for years."

"You've heard just the half of it. Because of the screwup, I told Marko that no orders were to go out unless I signed them off. That way we'll have proof if these high-maintenance customers like Big Bob try to grind us."

"So you handled the complaint, then put in a policy. What do you need from me?"

"Marko didn't take the rest of the order over to Big Bob. I promised Bob that it would be delivered before the end of the day. Marko had the order ready but sat on it. Then he told Big Bob that *I* was the one holding things up. I could have decked him."

"I don't understand."

"No one with any common sense would understand that guy. I was in a meeting with Clyde that afternoon and Marko left the order form on my desk. I didn't see it until the office was closing at 5:00. When I found out the order hadn't gone, I went ballistic and told him to stop playing games. All he did was wave a copy of my e-mail about the new signing-off procedure and tell me, 'Read your own e-

"Read your own e-mail, Mr. Manager."

mail, Mr. Manager. You didn't sign off the order yet.' He knew I wanted him to send out the order. Instead he set me up. I will not stand around and let my people stab me in the back and cost us customers. He's got to go."

"Well, no argument from me that something needs to change here. Clearly we have to put the customers first. On the other hand, we can't fire someone for following written procedure. Sounds like Marko was pretty steamed over the mix-up. What happened when you met with him right after the call from Big Bob?"

"He tried to give me this load about the courier coming early and taking the order while he was on his break — before he finished pulling it. I wasn't buying it for a minute. I told him, 'Don't pass the buck. You're the shipper and it's your signature on the waybill.' He got so ticked off he wasn't hearing anything I was saying, so I told him the meeting was over and I'd spell out the new procedure in an e-mail."

WHAT CAUSED THE WOBBLE?

The outcome of Doug and Marko's altercation could be described as wobbly at best. What role did each of the three legs of conflict play in this confrontation? The *problem* seemed straightforward enough: how to ensure orders were complete and verified before they were shipped. Yet Doug and Marko were unable to even agree there was a problem before the conversation broke down. Doug ended up imposing a solution to which Marko was clearly not committed. Marko followed the procedure to the letter, but ignored its spirit and intent. At the end of the day, the customer was not served and everyone lost.

The *process* could best be described as antagonistic, aggressive, and defensive. Neither person listened and the conversation became a ping-pong game of attack and defend, blame and deny. As a result, they failed to identify the problem, much less create a willingness to work on it together. Because Marko had no input into the solution Doug imposed, he had no investment in making it work. On the contrary, he felt justice was served when the situation blew up in Doug's face. In Marko's mind, Doug was the villain and deserved to be punished for his offensive behavior. Doug, on the other hand, saw Marko's lack of cooperation as additional evidence that Marko was the villain and himself the innocent victim. Until this situation was addressed, their animosity would poison their working relationship and spread discomfort throughout the organization.

Finally, neither Doug nor Marko managed his own *emotions,* and neither listened enough to build any degree of empathy. Ultimately, their unmanaged anger caused communication to break down.

Contrast Doug and Marko's situation with effective problem-solving relationships in your own life — ones in which you and the other person seem able to take any problem or conflict in stride. You find yourselves able to identify problems and willing to work toward solutions together. Such effective problem-solving relationships are characterized by most of the following:

- respect and trust
- willingness to listen and communicate
- commitment to a common goal
- flexibility and creativity

I believe we can all be exceptionally creative problem solvers — when we choose to be. Yet this strength also can be a weakness if, in our fixation on solving the problem, we fail to first build a foundation of respect and communication. Without that foundation, the other person will continue to see themselves as the victim and us as the villain, and molehills will seem like mountains. Even if we personally strive to solve the problem, we may find ourselves alone in that pursuit if respect and communication are lacking.

Diagnosing resistance

A manufacturer was troubled by a malfunction in a complex machine. A repair person came to the factory, looked at the machinery for a couple of minutes, then tapped the machine several times with a hammer. The factory manager's initial relief turned to dismay when a bill for $1,000 appeared. The flabbergasted manager demanded that the bill be itemized, since the service call took less than an hour and the machine was fixed with only a few taps. The following day, the manager received the itemized invoice. It read: "Tapping to repair machine: $10.00. Knowing where to tap: $990.00." And so it is when we are dealing with resistance in conflict. Knowing where to apply our efforts is critical.

Identifying the problem

Consider the problem as the meat and potatoes of the conflict. Ask yourself: what issue do we need to resolve? what topic to discuss? In the conflict between Dinah and Clyde in the previous chapter, for example, they needed to clarify who would book the boardroom and to discuss Dinah's workload and what support she required. They also needed to talk about how Clyde made decisions and how they would communicate in the future.

These issues were relatively easy to resolve once Dinah and Clyde began to communicate, clarify assumptions, and demonstrate respect for each other. Until then they were mired in conflict and unable to define the problem, much less solve it.

Chapter 11 provides examples of the many types of issues around which both workplace and personal conflicts arise.

Respecting process needs

The process refers to how we treat each other in conflict. Our need to feel respected is fundamental. When we feel disrespected, we see ourselves as the victim and cannot help but view those who disrespect us as the villain. And when we view the other as the villain, we are unlikely to trust or cooperate with them. Conversely, if the other person does not feel respected by us, they will see us as the villain. In this climate, the lack of cooperation and communication can cause even simple issues to become sticking points.

These *process needs* are a subset of the needs identified by Maslow and outlined in Chapter 3. To identify them, think of how you would want to be treated by another person — even when they disagree with you or are unable to give you what you want. Here are some common process needs.

To be heard and understood

The simplest way to show another person respect is to listen to them — to hear their story without interrupting or judging. One of the greatest compliments I received during my career as an insurance regulator came from the manager of a company with a very aggressive philosophy that generated numerous complaints. Given our somewhat adversarial relationship, I was surprised when he dropped by my office during my last week on the job and told me he'd be sorry to see me go. "We seldom agreed," he said, "but you always made time to hear me out. Thanks — I'll miss that."

When someone genuinely listens and attempts to understand our situation or perspective, it is hard to continue to see them as a villain. After all, villains are selfish and uncaring and are not the sort to show concern for someone else. Listening to another person is a powerful way to move beyond victims and villains toward cooperation.

TO HAVE OPTIONS AND CHOICES

People resent being forced to do anything. As discussed in Chapter 2, autonomy is a fundamental human need. When a decision is forced upon us, we often resist it not so much because we disagree with the decision as because we had no say in it. When we are presented with choices, we feel a sense of power (however limited) and are more likely to accept the final outcome.

Providing choices is a particularly effective strategy in situations when some aspect of the problem is non-negotiable. Most people in organizations operate under collective agreements, health and safety regulations, and internal policies and procedures. Sometimes these are "givens" and not open for negotiation. We may be limited to negotiating the "how" or the "when" rather than the "if." Even in families and personal relationships, you may not be willing or able to negotiate certain issues. Yet there still may be ways to involve the other person and provide them with a sense of autonomy.

When my daughter was two years old, bedtime was a struggle. My wife and I were not willing to negotiate bedtime each night, and 8:00 became a given. One night, this normally cooperative (and, from a father's perspective, angelic) child decided to test her independence and declared, "I'm not going." After several unsuccessful attempts to reason with her, I called upon the parenting tips I had received and provided her with a choice. The choice was not around the "if," but around the "how." I asked her whether she would like to walk to her room on her own or whether she wanted me to give her a ride.

She obviously hadn't read the same parenting books I had, for she stuck out her bottom lip and reiterated, "I'm not going." I drew a deep breath, struggled to stay in my "happy place," and said, "Sounds like you don't want to walk. Why don't I give you a ride?" With that I picked her up. Fortunately, I held her at arm's length and managed to avoid a very personal injury from her predictable flailing as she demanded I put her down. I did so, stepped back, and observed, "You want to walk to your room on your own — that's fine." At that, she glared at me, puffed up her chest like a bantam rooster, and defiantly strutted down the hall to her bedroom, muttering, "I'll — walk — by — my — self." Within a minute she was in her bedroom, feeling she had won a victory.

Even when the choice may seem obvious, the subtle sense of autonomy that comes with a choice allows a person to save face and often defuses resistance. Villains control and deprive. When someone provides us with a choice, we are less likely to view them as the villain and more likely to work with them on the problem.

To be given reasons

Nothing shuts down communication like the brick wall of a position. When people are confronted by a position, they tend to respond in kind. Flexibility and creativity fall by the wayside. This is especially true when rules and regulations are involved — the "givens" discussed above. Phrases like "because it's the policy" or "that's just the way it is" trigger feelings of powerlessness that fuel frustration and anger.

Even when a policy is not up for negotiation, it is helpful to spend some time outlining the reasoning behind the policy and discussing what it is intended to achieve. By focusing on the spirit rather than the letter of the law, we may be able to provide ways for the other person to achieve their goals within the policy.

Positions trap us on the drama triangle. Someone who tells us "the way it should be" and ignores our interests exhibits the control we associate with the role of the villain. As we push back, they likely experience us in the same way. Emphasizing reasons encourages a flexibility that moves us beyond the right and wrong that characterize the drama triangle.

TO BE TREATED FAIRLY

Nothing casts us in the role of victim as quickly as the perception of unfair treatment. As children, we may complain that our sibling has more raisins in their rice pudding. We may object to a household rule because "Fred doesn't have to go to bed at 8:00." And those who treat us unfairly must be villains.

Of course, fairness, like beauty, is in the eye of the beholder. Almost everyone in conflict claims they want only what is fair and will then spend hours arguing about whose idea of fairness is right. One way around this impasse is to introduce objective criteria and independent standards. We may refer to "the going rate," accepted industry practices, precedent, or other comparables. What do others do or charge in similar situations? We could even ask an independent expert to provide an impartial valuation. All of these techniques seek to break the deadlock of personal opinion in a way that both parties would consider fair.

In examining the conflict between Doug and Marko, it's not hard to see why communication broke down. Doug didn't take the time to listen to or understand Marko's perspective, didn't explain the reasons for creating a new policy, offered Marko no options, and handed down his decree in a way that Marko felt was unfair. In the absence of a respectful process, Marko became angry and clammed up. Even though Doug had the power to impose the new policy, Marko was far from committed to it. As a result, he followed the policy to the letter to the detriment of the customer.

Stabilizing the emotion

Unmanaged emotion blinds us to reason and shuts down communication. Most often, anger and frustration stem from the process leg of conflict because the perception of disrespect is so immediate. With the other person literally in our face, we may not have the opportunity to take a breath and manage ourselves.

Other times, the problem itself is emotionally charged, as in discussions about children or a core value. Still other times, anger may be unrelated to either the problem or the process. People may bring their "baggage" to a situation. Because we never can know their full story, all we experience is their overreaction to a simple issue or an innocuous comment.

Anger or frustration, regardless of the cause, hinders both discussion and resolution. When we are angry, we don't listen. (Well, we might listen just enough to make the other person wrong.) We seldom articulate our point of view effectively. (Yelling "Now you just listen to me for one minute" does not qualify.) And problem solving seldom progresses beyond suggesting that the target of our anger knows what they can do with their idea.

Accordingly, emotion is the wobbliest "leg" of the stool and the most likely place to find the source of resistance. If we fail to manage our own emotion, we will find it difficult to respect the other person and can easily act like a villain. If we do not defuse the other person's emotion, we can expect a long and uphill battle.

Generally, people who are angry need time and space — a chance to vent, tell their story, and blow off steam. You could view this as letting the air out of a balloon. We also can defuse a person's emotion by demonstrating understanding (Doug could have acknowledged to Marko that "Big Bob sure can be a pain when he gets upset"). Although we may be more comfortable focusing on facts, we won't get very far until we have stabilized emotion. Chapter 7 expands on the dynamics of anger, Chapter 8 focuses on managing our own emotion, and Chapter 9 provides strategies to defuse another person's anger.

Big Bob goes bananas (revisited)
DIAGNOSING MARKO'S RESISTANCE

Let's see how the three legs of conflict applied to Doug and Marko's situation. Doug and Marko had to figure out how to dispatch orders efficiently and verify them as complete. This was by no means an insurmountable problem. Two calm and reasonable people likely could generate several workable solutions. Yet two intelligent and experienced employees became so angry and defensive that they couldn't even define the problem, much less solve it. What got in the way?

Doug had just been blasted by Big Bob on the phone when he approached Marko. Doug failed to manage his own anger and was unprepared to listen to Marko during their meeting. Marko, in turn, felt attacked and disrespected, and his anger rose. He was already upset by *his* encounter with Big Bob, and Doug's accusations touched an already raw nerve. Their combined anger quickly transformed a conversation into a confrontation, leaving no room for reason, information, or options. Marko emerged from the meeting feeling steamrollered. He didn't challenge his boss head on, but later undermined Doug by applying the policy literally and to the detriment of the customer. This type of passive-aggressive behavior often results when someone feels overpowered and too intimidated to raise concerns directly.

DOUG TRIES AGAIN

Doug spent considerable time with Gale, during which she worked with him to identify the resistance and plan a different approach. Doug decided to give it a second try.

Doug hears a knock on his office door and takes a deep breath as an impassive Marko stares down at him. "Thanks, Marko. I guess you got my message about wanting to talk about the Big Bob mix-up. You got 15 minutes to walk?"

Marko eyes Doug suspiciously for a few seconds, then grunts and follows Doug out the back door. "What do you want now?"

"First, I want to apol ..." Doug slows and draws a breath as the word sticks in his throat. "Look, I was pretty steamed yesterday and didn't hear your side of things. What I want to do is look at what happened and see how we can make sure it doesn't happen again."

Marko still looks somewhat suspicious. "You didn't care about my side yesterday."

"I know. Tell you what — I'll shut up, you tell me what happened with Big Bob, then I'll tell you my side. How does that sound?"

"Do I need Lance here?"

"No. No discipline, no blame. Just sorting things out. Can you start from the beginning for me?"

Marko looks skeptical, but decides to give it a shot. "Well, we all know Big Bob is picky, so I pulled his order first. Except that fancy new banana stuff wasn't in yet. Lance says it's coming by 10:30, so I take my coffee early so I can finish the order when it gets in. But the courier guy picks up the order while I'm away. The next thing I know, Big Bob is screaming on the phone about being cheated. Well, nobody calls me a liar, so I told him to settle down. Then he goes ballistic and threatens to call you and get me fired. I told him to take his best shot and hung up."

"Big Bob sure can be a pain when he gets upset."

"You got that right. He didn't even listen when I told him I'd deliver his precious Banana Blend the next morning."

"So you had the order picked, except for the product that wasn't in. Then the courier took it before you finished."

"You got it."

"Thanks — now things make more sense. Let me tell you what concerns me here. First, I want to make sure the courier does-n't take any orders before they're complete. Second, I need some way to prove we've

"Then he threatens to call you and get me fired."

sent the whole order in case there are mix-ups with customers. Big Bob had two guys check the order when it arrived, so I was firing blanks when he came after us. We need to be able to prove the orders we send are complete."

"I can talk to the courier company. I think they had some new guy on."

"That's a good start. Where do you keep the orders that aren't complete yet?"

"With the other orders, except they got no packing slip. Those guys know that."

"What if you kept the incomplete orders separate from the others?"

"Then I got to move the stuff twice. Takes too long."

"What else do you think we could do?"

Marko briefly ponders Doug's question.

"I could put signs on the pallets. Green for go, red for stop. Even those dummies at the courier could figure that out."

"Sounds like it's worth a try. Now how can we prove that we sent out complete orders? I want to back you guys up, but I need to have some proof to go to bat for you when a customer complains. But now that I think about it, it's crazy to have me sign off everything when I'm in so many meetings. What about getting Lance to check the order and initial it next to you?"

"Fine, as long as he's around."

"The important thing is to have someone take a quick look at the order and verify it. Hey — how about Melanie when Lance isn't around? She could always squeeze in five minutes. And she's so nice, even Big Bob would trust her."

Marko hesitates and begins to brighten at the prospect of dealing with Lance and Melanie instead of Doug. "Sounds good to me. How you going to fix it up with Big Bob?"

"I'll phone him, then send him a letter when we've made our changes. He's an important customer, so it'll have to be a nice, diplomatic one."

Marko smiles for the first time. "You'd better let Gale write it, then."

"You'd better let Gale write it, then."

Doug's laugh and nod signal an end to the meeting. "Even better, Marko, even better. I'll check with Lance and Melanie to make sure this works for them, then e-mail everyone to keep them in the loop. You talk to the courier guys and tell them we're trying out the color-coding. Thanks."

This example demonstrates the value of listening to someone else's conflict story. When we do, we stabilize all three legs of the conflict and lay a solid foundation on which to build a lasting resolution. Chapter 14 provides a framework to help us do this.

Summary

We don't see the other person as the villain because they disagree with us; we see them as the villain because of how they treat us.

Conflict is like a three-legged stool, encompassing the problem, the process, and the emotions. When you encounter resistance, refrain from the urge to push harder against the problem itself. Instead, take a moment to step back and check each of the three legs of conflict. Start by taking the emotional temperature — your own and the other person's. Then assess whether each of you feels heard and respected in the conversation. Once you've stabilized those legs, then apply your efforts to the problem itself.

Often, taking a moment to summarize your understanding of the other person's perspective can work wonders to break a deadlock and open communication.

From theory to practice

Consider a conflict you recently witnessed or heard about and examine the source of the resistance. In what way did each of the following play a role?

- the problem
- the process
- the emotions

What might either person have done to move past the resistance toward a cooperative solution?

CHAPTER 7

THE PERILS OF ANGER MOUNTAIN

You can't shake hands with a clenched fist.
— Indira Gandhi

Anger and conflict go hand in hand. And as outlined in Chapter 6, unmanaged emotion will block communication and prevent resolution. Anger is simply energy. It is a catalyst — a call to action. Our choice lies in how we answer that call.

When something or someone triggers our anger, we impulsively protect ourselves through a response of fight or flight. If we choose to fight, we play the role of a hero who protects the innocent (usually ourselves) and confronts the evildoer. Our anger, however, can push us over the fine line between hero and villain. A self-righteous attitude that "they have it coming" drives us to punish the other person. We can easily find ourselves engaging in behaviors normally associated with the villain role: personal attacks, threats, yelling, and inappropriate use of the middle finger.

Anger also motivates other people to behave in ways we find objectionable. Yet, flushed with righteousness, they are convinced they are the hero and their actions are justified. It's easy to see how we can fall into the pattern of attack and counterattack that characterizes confrontation. This chapter both explains how anger leads to confrontation and provides ways to respond productively to anger.

Responses to anger

When confronted with a threat, most creatures rely on one of three methods of survival: fight, flight, or freeze. Human beings are no different. As discussed in Chapter 3, these responses are motivated by what Maslow identified as our basic needs for survival and safety. In the face of a physical threat or survival situation, these reactions are not only appropriate — they are essential.

Fortunately, we seldom find ourselves physically threatened or battling for survival. The organizational and family jungles we inhabit are more likely to present psychological threats and verbal attacks. Regrettably, we do not instinctively differentiate between physical threats, where fight or flight is necessary, and psychological ones, in which those same impulses are counterproductive.

If someone insults or slights us during a meeting, for example, we might respond in kind by insulting or even threatening them. The resulting escalation diverts us from the issue at hand. Conversely, if we succumb to our flight response we might leave the meeting or, more typically, if we freeze we may stay and shut down ("Whatever"). By choosing a flight or a freeze response, we condone the other person's inappropriate behavior and will be treated the way we allow them to treat us. Additionally, whatever issue sparked the attack likely will fester. Such avoidance often leads to passive-aggressive behavior such as gossip or sabotage. In short, what may be an appropriate response to a physical threat is unlikely to be helpful in the face of a verbal or psychological attack. To collaborate, we must develop other responses. Let's start by looking at how anger affects our body and our mind.

The diagram on the next page reflects what happens in our body and mind when we become angry. In general terms, a perceived threat initiates a survival reaction in our body, at the expense of our ability to reason and communicate.

WE GET TRIGGERED

A trigger is a perceived threat or attack. It may be a physical threat, but more likely it will be a verbal or psychological one. Sometimes it may be a single remark or event; other times it may be the "straw that broke the camel's back." The trigger is the point in our story when "the knife goes in" and we feel victimized. The words and behaviors that set us off usually are linked to previous experience — they "trigger" feelings that already exist within us. Triggers may be external (a look, a word, or an action) or internal (what we think about or tell ourselves). Consider how often we replay incidents in our mind or retell a story in which we were wronged. Each time we relive the event, we re-experience the emotions attached to it ("Just thinking about it makes me angry").

FIGURE 7A: ANGER AROUSAL CYCLE

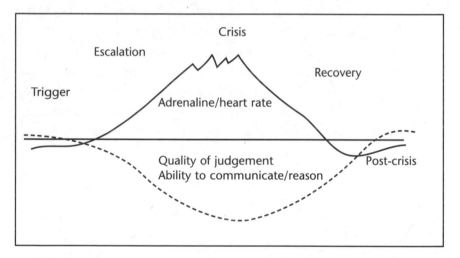

Our physical and emotional condition also contributes to our sensitivity to certain triggers. When we are tired or hungry, we often find ourselves irritated by relatively minor events. When we are frustrated or in doubt, we may react to a comment that we normally would take in stride.

Consider how Vic Tom reacted at Turm-Oil's quarterly meeting. During the discussion about the decline in sales, many comments triggered Vic until he eventually went ballistic. The decline in sales was already a sore spot for him. Given his history of conflict with his co-workers, he likely had marshaled his defense well before the meeting even started. His sensitivity caused him to respond defensively to what he perceived as accusations and attacks. Here are some behaviors, comments, and thoughts that triggered Vic during the meeting:

- the glare from Clyde (external)
- the threat by Clyde that "something will change" (external)
- recalling previous lack of support (internal)
- recalling the cut to his travel budget (internal)
- Dean telling him to "send me an email" (external)
- revisiting the lack of stock and errors in shipping (internal)
- remembering the absence of brochures for the trade show (internal)
- and finally, Dinah describing his delay in approving the brochure as "stupidity" (external)

Vic was in no state to recognize these specific triggers or choose how to respond to them. Instead, he reacted angrily and emotional-

ly to each, accelerating his ascent of anger mountain until, fully in the crisis stage, he stormed from the room.

Triggered

OUR BODY ESCALATES

During the escalation phase the body readies itself for action as adrenaline and other energizing chemicals are released into the blood. Physically, breathing becomes rapid and shallow, the heart pounds, blood pressure increases, and muscles tense (especially in the jaw, shoulders, hands, chest, and throat). As a result of this muscle tightness, the voice becomes strained and higher pitched. These physical indicators also can warn us when another person is becoming angry. During this phase we retain some ability to think and reason, though not for long.

As Vic's anger escalated, his voice began to rise, his facial muscles tightened, and his eyes widened. This is when he began to shift from reason to personal attacks.

Escalating

WE HIT CRISIS

In certain situations, escalation can progress to crisis, commonly referred to as "seeing red" or the volcano atop anger mountain. This stage is characterized by an overwhelming rush of adrenaline that demands "fight" or "flight." We become so focused on our adversary that we develop tunnel vision and are unable to hear. Our ability to think, reason, and communicate is minimal.

As Vic's confrontation with the rest of the staff escalated, he quickly became so angry he was no longer able to articulate his concerns and resorted to slamming his briefcase shut and storming from the room while sputtering to himself.

In crisis

WE GRADUALLY RECOVER

During the recovery stage, the adrenaline and other chemicals dissipate and oxygen begins to find its way to our forebrain. The rate at which people recover depends on their physiological and psychological makeup as well as the intensity of their response to the situation. Some people may recover within minutes, while others may take hours to let go of their anger and its symptoms. This difference explains why people will not always respond immediately to our best efforts to defuse them. A truck careening down a hill takes time to stop, even when the brakes are applied. The time it takes to stop will depend on the size of the truck, the slope of the hill, and the condition of the road. Similarly, the degree of anger, a person's makeup, and the environment all contribute to the time it takes someone to calm down. When attempting to defuse someone else's anger, be patient and hang in there, even if your efforts don't produce immediate results.

Recovering

In Vic's case, his recovery took place in the solitude of the parking lot. Because his eruption had been so long coming, it took him a good half-hour to calm down enough that he could rejoin the meeting.

POST-CRISIS GUILT AND DEPRESSION

What goes up must come down, and in the post-crisis stage the heart rate drops below normal as the body reacts to the earlier chemical rush. As reason returns, we reflect on our actions. In escalation and crisis, we see the other person as an unequivocal villain, deserving of everything we can throw at them. In post-crisis, we examine our own behavior and often feel guilty or even depressed about the way we reacted. These feelings can cause us to avoid the other person or refrain from revisiting the issue. Issues get buried, only to be retriggered in the future. Alternatively, our desire to soothe our guilt may spur us to uncondi- tionally surrender, only to subsequently chafe under an unfair agreement.

In our example, Vic calmed down in the parking lot, shaken by the intensity of emotion the meeting had sparked in him. When he returned to the meeting, his embarrassment and exhaustion prevented him from effectively advocating for himself.

Post-crisis

Significance of the anger arousal cycle

When the concept of anger mountain was presented to a class of ele- mentary school students, one boy grasped the concept immediately. "So you mean that the madder we get, the stupider we get?" he asked. From the mouths of babes …

Understanding the anger arousal cycle helps us manage conflict in a couple of ways. First, it can help us manage ourselves. By know- ing our triggers and impulses, we can develop strategies to respond more effectively when triggered. Such strategies can help us curb the self-righteousness that fuels the hero role and sends us into attack mode, causing the other person to experience us as the angry villain. The following chapter provides more specific tools and strategies to manage our own anger.

Second, we can deal more effectively with someone else who is angry if we remember how little oxygen is making its way to their forebrain. No wonder they are having difficulty communicating or problem solving. I repeatedly see people in conflict make the mistake of attempting to reason with someone who is atop anger mountain. Their arguments and suggestions, however logical, are not heard by the other person. We do better if we can defuse the anger before focusing on the problem at hand.

Strategies to defuse others' anger

Anger often occurs in situations in which people feel confused, powerless, or discounted. These feelings often describe people's experiences in dealing with bureaucracy: confused by red tape, powerless and discounted in the face of "the system." To defuse someone's anger, we can create an environment that provides them with a sense of clarity, choice, and connection.

Defusing anger is as much an art as a science. Basic principles and tools certainly apply, though people respond differently. The more tools in our toolbox, the better. Don't worry if one approach doesn't seem to work; simply try another. Any effort will at least convey, at some level, your intent to understand the other person's story and work with them. Your effort begins to erode their view of you as the villain, for villains are selfish and inconsiderate, not empathetic. Over time, we can influence how others see us in conflict.

The following strategies to defuse anger start with those most likely to work with someone at their angriest. In the crisis stage, for example, a person is unable to hear or comprehend more than a basic idea or single word. As they start to descend anger mountain, we can then begin to use strategies that require them to think and communicate (such as an open-ended question).

Because anger is physiological, don't expect someone to respond immediately to your attempts to defuse it. Their anger is a wave of energy, so find ways to connect with them as they ride out the wave. This will take time and may require you to use many tools before the person is able to communicate effectively.

GIVE THEM THEIR "ONE MINUTE"

The term "giving someone their one minute" was coined by Danaan Parry, author of *Warriors of the Heart* and founder of the Earthstewards Network. "Giving them their one minute" means listening to someone with genuine curiosity, putting our own story and judgments temporarily aside to allow us to listen deeply. This is a powerful concept in defusing anger, for sometimes what we don't do is more important than what we do. In attempting to connect with the angry person, we may only trigger them further, especially if we interrupt them to justify or defend ourselves. As instinctive as this may feel, it serves only to fuel their anger because we are competing with their story. Such interruptions often prompt the other person to tell their story over again, only more loudly to ensure we get the point.

Nonverbal communication can be key in the beginning. Someone who is angry will respond more to body language and tone of voice than to words. Facing them will show concern and attention. Stand at an angle, however, so as not to be perceived as challenging them head-on. Avoid crossing your arms or placing your hands on your hips, as these gestures may imply that you are closed to their perspective. We can demonstrate concern and attention through eye contact and nodding. (Make sure your eyes are open when you nod.)

As with any conflict strategy, we need to continually assess the effectiveness of our silence. Often, the other person will "run out of steam" and begin to express themselves more calmly. In other cases, however, they may interpret our silence as indifference and become even more animated in an attempt to make their point. We also need to remain aware of the impact of their anger on us. As we listen, we may need to set limits to ensure we are not personally abused as they vent: "I can see you're angry. I'm not willing to be sworn at. Tell me your concerns without the swearing." Or "Cool it with the personal attacks. Give me exactly what happened." Chapter 13 addresses how we can stand up for ourselves assertively.

At the end of one workshop, a participant vowed to "give everyone their 'one minute' — unless they're upset; then I'll give them two minutes." Had the staff at Turm-Oil Inc. employed this approach, Vic likely would have been able to express his frustration and focus on the details of the problem. Instead, their collective attempts to justify, blame, and defend simply stoked Vic's anger and ensured the meeting would be memorable, though unproductive.

CREATE SPEED BUMPS

Speed bumps are short interjections intended both to connect with the speaker and to break their momentum. An angry person who gets no reaction may feel unacknowledged and repeat themselves even more loudly. Paradoxically, although they require acknowledgment, they are neither able nor inclined to listen to us for more than a second or two.

People often respond to hearing their name repeated several times. This simple act of recognition can gain us a moment or two as we attempt to focus the conversation on their specific concerns. Alternatively, restating key words in their diatribe also serves to slow their pace and encourages them to elaborate on their concerns. This tool is especially valuable when someone is getting wound up and approaching their crisis point. In that state, they respond as much to the tone of our voice as to our words. Unless we match their intensity (though not necessarily their volume), they are unlikely to respond.

Had Dinah attempted to use this approach as Vic neared his snapping point, she might have forcefully repeated his name, "Vic ...Vic ... VIC," to break his momentum and get his attention. Or she might have picked up on a key word or two, such as "brochures?" or "trade show?" Hearing those, Vic would have been more than happy to elaborate on his grievances, perhaps in a more productive manner.

SHOW EMPATHY

Empathy involves understanding and acknowledging another's feelings. It flows when we attempt to put ourselves in another person's shoes and identify with their feelings and perspective. We cannot know how they feel, only make an educated guess and check it out with them. But we need to do more than simply claim we understand — we need to demonstrate that understanding. Telling someone "I know how you feel" is a sure-fire way to hasten their climb up anger mountain. They will not hesitate to let us know that we *don't* know how they feel because we're not the victim here.

We can demonstrate empathy by reflecting the emotion we sense in another. We don't even have to be perfect, as long as we are genuine. People in conflict have a story to tell. If they sense we are attempting to understand, they will clarify whatever we may have missed.

Had Perry decided to empathize with Vic during the quarterly meeting, he might have said something like: "Vic, I realize how stressful the budget cuts were for you" or "Sounds as if you feel like you're being set up as the fall guy here."

Whether these comments were 100 percent accurate would not have mattered. If Perry's response had missed the mark, Vic would have let him know and clarified how he was feeling and why. If Perry had been on target, Vic likely would have taken the opportunity to elaborate: "Sure I feel blamed. We're a team when everything is rosy, but I'm the bad guy when things go south." This reply could have served as a starting point for the group to fully understand Vic's concerns and identify the problem.

VALIDATE THEIR EXPERIENCE

Empathy focuses on the other person's feelings; validation focuses on a more universal experience. Validation acknowledges that a person's anger is normal and understandable in the circumstances. This focus can reduce the other person's feelings of disconnection and demonstrate our understanding of their situation.

In our example, Vic expounded on the number of customer complaints arising from computer system glitches. Dean could have normalized Vic's frustration by acknowledging that "new software can be a real pain. I don't blame you for being ticked off."

PARAPHRASE KEY CONCERNS

A paraphrase reflects a speaker's key words and attempts to capture the gist of their story. This tool is particularly useful when someone is in the foothills of anger mountain and is willing to let you try to clarify what you heard. (People who are extremely angry, however, are unlikely to give us time to paraphrase without interrupting us and continuing to vent.)

Had Clyde chosen to defuse Vic early in the discussion of the sales figures, he might have said something like: "So let me make sure I understand you. You see the sales figures reflecting a number of factors, including distribution and budget."

As with empathetic statements, we don't have to be 100 percent accurate when we paraphrase another person. If Clyde had misinterpreted something, Vic would have taken the opportunity to clarify what he *did* mean. If Vic had felt Clyde captured the essence of his concerns, he might have been encouraged to expand by saying something such as: "Exactly. I've been going full out, but this problem goes well beyond sales." The door to problem solving would have been opened, albeit only a crack.

ASK OPEN-ENDED QUESTIONS

Open-ended questions, covered in more detail in Chapter 12, invite people to express their concerns instead of raging. However, people must have enough oxygen available to their forebrain to be able to formulate a coherent answer. If you ask someone who is atop anger mountain, "What's the problem?" their answer is unlikely to be either helpful or pretty.

Questions that help you trace the person's story back to their trigger are invaluable in this context. Had Dean, for example, not frozen during the heated exchange involving Vic and Doug, he might have asked, "What specifically is the problem with the new software?" or "When is this most problematic for you?" or simply "What happened?"

REFRAME TO FOCUS ON UNMET NEEDS

At the root of a person's conflict story, at the point when "the knife went in," lie unmet needs. People in conflict are often so angry that they rail against other people, blind to their own needs. We can move the conversation forward by reframing their story to focus on their needs and preferred future. This is not about changing or interpreting their story, but about viewing it through a more productive lens.

This approach requires a willingness on the other person's part to listen to us and reflect on the accuracy of our reframing. It is unlikely to be effective with someone who still feels the need to vent their anger. When you have defused the other person enough to win a hearing, however, an accurate reframing will dramatically shift the tenor of the conversation from attack and defense to understanding. When someone feels heard at this deeper level, they often will relax their shoulders and lower their voice, as they no longer feel the need to yell in order to be heard.

If any of those attending the quarterly meeting had chosen to reflect Vic's unmet needs, they might have said something like this: "Vic, what I'm getting is that you need to be able to count on our support in your marketing efforts. You need to know that existing customers will have their orders filled accurately and be treated well." Though Vic undoubtedly would have had more to say on the subject, his tone and comments likely would have softened when he heard his needs identified and acknowledged.

SUMMARIZE THE BIG PICTURE

A summary pulls together our understanding of the other person's story. It can help us determine whether the other person feels sufficiently understood to give us a hearing and work together on the problem. A summary focuses on the highlights of their story and invites the other person to clarify anything we might have missed. It is a good way to take the emotional temperature. Their response will let us assess whether they would be willing to listen to our perspective or consider possible solutions.

The time and place for apologies

Genuine apologies have their place in conflict resolution but have been so overused that their effectiveness is limited. "I'm sorry," for example, seems to be an automatic reaction to another's anger or frustration. Some people say "I'm sorry" when someone else bumps into them. Other times, an apology is offered before someone has even finished their story. An apology often is interpreted as "Don't be mad anymore; I said I'm sorry." When we feel wronged and have a story to tell, we have little patience with someone implying we shouldn't be mad anymore. People may be made even angrier by an immediate apology and respond with something like: "If you were sorry, you wouldn't have done that in the first place."

It also may be that you have nothing to apologize for — you did nothing wrong. Their anger may be misdirected or based on inaccurate or incomplete information. In those cases, the other person may see your apology as a sign of weakness and expect unconditional surrender, making them even more difficult to deal with.

When we think about it, "I'm sorry" speaks more to our intention than to the impact on the other person. It diverts the spotlight from their story to ours and often is followed by "but I only meant ..." If you have made a mistake, you may find it more effective to say, "You're right. You should have been included in that decision" than "I'm sorry you weren't included." In short, what follows "I'm sorry" is much more important than the words themselves.

With an apology or any of these tools, being genuine is more important than being accurate. Ralph Waldo Emerson said, "What you are stands over you the while, and thunders so that I cannot hear what you say to the contrary." A lack of sincerity reduces these powerful tools to manipulation, more likely to trigger another person's anger than to defuse it.

Summary

We react instinctively to a perceived attack with a fight, flight, or freeze response. A fight response places us squarely on the drama triangle of confrontation as either a hero or a villain. A flight or freeze response assigns us the role of victim.

By knowing ourselves and our triggers, we can develop strategies to respond effectively.

As our bodies ramp up for fight or flight, our ability to communicate and reason declines. Similarly, when someone else is angry, they will be unable to rationally problem solve with us. Remember to defuse the anger before delving into the problem at hand.

The more tools you have to defuse someone else's anger, the better. Here are some basic ones:

- Give them their "one minute"
- Create speed bumps
- Show empathy
- Validate their experience
- Paraphrase key concerns
- Ask open-ended questions
- Reframe to focus on their unmet needs
- Summarize the big picture

From theory to practice

Watch for signs of anger in others throughout your day. When you observe someone who is angry, ask yourself:

- What triggered them? What threat or attack might they have perceived?
- How did others respond to their anger?
- What did others do that helped defuse their anger?
- What did others do that didn't help or even made them angrier?

CHAPTER 8

BEWARE THE CONFLICT GREMLINS

If you can keep your head when all about you
Are losing theirs and blaming it on you;
If you can trust yourself when all men doubt you,
But make allowance for their doubting, too ...
— Rudyard Kipling

At our best, in conflict we remain calm and focused. We size up the situation and choose an appropriate approach, tool, or strategy. At our worst, we react impulsively and say giddy-up to our mouths before our minds are hitched up. This impulsive reaction is not surprising; as we have seen, our survival instinct is for fight or flight, both of which put us squarely back on the drama triangle as hero or victim. Even though we may have many communication skills at our disposal, old coping habits die hard and often trigger immediate defensive responses.

Strategies to manage our own anger

Susan Scott, in her excellent book *Fierce Conversations,* says, "All conversations are with ourselves, and some may involve other people." Rather than worrying about and judging the other person in conflict, we can apply that energy more productively to understanding and managing our own reactions. This chapter provides insights and strategies to help us remain productive during conflict. The foundation for change is awareness: of our triggers, our breathing, our body, our feelings, and our thoughts.

KNOW YOUR TRIGGERS

We can begin this process of awareness by identifying our triggers. Why do certain people, mannerisms, or behaviors trigger us (but don't necessarily trigger other people)? When and with whom are these behaviors most likely to trigger us? Knowing ourselves and our triggers allows us to develop a preventive maintenance program that can serve us when conflict surfaces.

Part of our maintenance program can involve reducing the size of our "hot buttons" and making them more difficult for others to push. Police officers, frontline government employees, and computer help-line operators normally develop thick skins and effective coping mechanisms because abuse, unfortunately, comes with their chosen vocations. They cannot avoid angry people and therefore must find ways to depersonalize verbal attacks and defuse and manage abusive situations. For those who fail to do so, the resultant stress and their own ineffectiveness usually have them looking for a new career.

REMEMBER TO BREATHE

As trite as this sounds, in conflict we often forget to breathe. As we feel attacked, we become tense and tend to either hold our breath or take short, shallow breaths. We become rigid, our energy blocked. If we can train ourselves to take a couple of deep breaths in response to conflict, we accomplish several things. First, we allow oxygen to circulate, some of which hopefully will arrive at our forebrain and awaken our communication and reasoning skills. Second, we begin to relax and allow energy to flow through us. This physical activity provides an alternative to the fight or flight response. And third, we buy ourselves some time and avoid counterproductive impulsive responses. With this choice comes a sense of power, even in an uncomfortable situation.

During a workshop with the staff of a high school, I asked participants about the benefits of breathing in the face of anger. The police liaison officer smiled and said, "As long as I'm breathing in, I'm not talking." That alone is a good enough reason to train ourselves to breathe when feeling triggered.

GROUND YOURSELF

The seemingly simple act of planting both feet on the ground and breathing deeply can empower us in times of stress and in the face of anger. As the traditional Eastern practices of meditation, tai chi, shiatsu, aikido, and yoga have grown in popularity in the West, we have become more aware of the energy in our bodies. These practices, in various ways, seek to ground us and focus our energy productively. Such training is invaluable in conflict.

Aikido refers to the *hara,* or power center; tai chi calls this the *dantian.* This energy reservoir provides a necessary sense of balance and inner security. Many people feel scattered and unbalanced in conflict and react accordingly. They either fall back (passively) or push forward (aggressively). They are unable to access a third alternative — an assertive stance in which people hold their ground, set limits, and focus on the problem.

Thomas Crum's book *The Magic of Conflict* uses aikido techniques to illustrate how to work with, rather than against, the energy of another person. Danaan Parry's *Warriors of the Heart* also refers to aikido principles and provides an exercise to help us find our "power center" — an ability that serves us well in conflict.

Get to know your gremlins

What's a good fairy tale without a gremlin or two to cause some mischief? In his wonderful book *Taming Your Gremlin,* Richard Carson uses the image of a "gremlin" to represent our unhelpful and even destructive inner voice. Carson defines a gremlin as "the narrator in your head" who "tells you who and how you are, and defines and interprets your every experience." The goal of the gremlin is for us to be unhappy. I've found I actually have a committee of gremlins in my head. (Okay, for the record, I don't hear little voices and, of course, neither do you. But if we did, what would they sound like?)

In applying Carson's work to conflict, I've discovered that we have specialized "conflict gremlins" whose sole purpose is to stop us from resolving conflicts productively. Our conflict gremlins come in all sizes and shapes and usually fall into one of two basic types — the "fight" gremlins and the "flight" gremlins. They urge us to respond to conflict either aggressively or passively, but not collaboratively.

MEET MRS. ROGERS AND BUZZ

I came face-to-face with my two main conflict gremlins in a pickup basketball game several years ago. In theory, we were a bunch of fifty-somethings out only for exercise, though any time men keep score, things seem to take on a life of their own. One evening, the teams we chose resulted in a mismatch in which the team I was on got walloped. I suggested we swap several players to restore a balance. A particularly competitive player on the other team (clearly the villain in my story) dismissed my suggestion.

That's when my "Mrs. Rogers" gremlin kicked in. She is the quintessential sweet, gray-haired elementary school teacher, the one you never wanted to disappoint. (I call her Mrs. Rogers because I think she probably would have been married to television's Mr. Rogers.) She told me to "play nice" and get along and I dutifully took the high road and didn't push the point. *I* would not stoop to arguing over such a petty issue. I was too big for that.

When the other team scored the first seven baskets of the next game, Mrs. Rogers was nowhere to be heard. Instead, another voice blared in my mind — that of Buzz. Buzz embodied the righteous indignation that would never allow such unfairness to go unchallenged. I found myself rallying to his cry that "we don't have to take this — we're out of here."

As I angrily strode toward the bench to gather my things I became aware of yet another voice. This voice seemed somewhat detached from the unfolding drama. "Whoa, whoa," it said. "Slow down — you've got some choices here." This broke my momentum enough for me to take stock of the situation. I realized I wouldn't feel good about myself if I stormed out, nor if I allowed myself to be steamrollered. I decided to stay and try to work things out. I chose the rather inelegant "This is garbage. This isn't working. I feel like walking out of here, but I don't want to do that."

Without going into boring details (resolution isn't nearly as exciting as conflict), we worked it out and enjoyed a good sweat for the rest of the evening. And a postscript: I later talked to the competitive "villain" on the other team about the incident and my reaction. During our conversation, we found we had a lot in common in terms of our reactions in conflict and we got to know each other at a whole new level.

FIGHT GREMLINS

"Fight" gremlins spur us to don the hero's mantle to defend ourselves, right the wrong, and vanquish the villain. They tell us things like:

"How dare they!"

"What a jerk."

"No way they're getting away with this."

"You don't have to take this."

Here are some fight gremlins that students in my workshops have identified over the years:

- a troll under a bridge, growing increasingly irritated by footsteps
- a reluctant Superman
- Mr. Worf (a Klingon from "Star Trek")
- the Incredible Hulk
- a bulldozer
- Raging Bull
- "George," a 6'4" gorilla with knuckles dragging
- a hand on my collar pushing me forward

These gremlins and their attack messages lock us into the role of hero on the drama triangle. We self-righteously focus on straightening out the other person instead of seeking to identify and solve the problem.

FLIGHT GREMLINS

Our "flight" gremlins push us into the role of victim. They proclaim our innocence and remind us of the futility of engaging in conflict. They reinforce our sense of powerlessness, telling us things such as:

"Get me out of here."

"Help — this isn't safe."

"Why bother? This isn't worth the hassle."

"You can't handle this. Run away while you have the chance."

Here are some examples of flight gremlins my students have identified over the years:

- Porky Pig (sputtering)
- Humpty Dumpty (ready to fall)
- Wily Coyote (the cartoon Roadrunner's fall guy)
- an island
- a Nervous Nellie bobbing in a rickety rowboat
- a wet tissue

TURM-OIL GREMLINS

Each Turm-Oil Inc. employee has his or her unique gremlin. (Well, they actually have several, but were willing to share only one with us.) Fortunately, through Gale Reasoner's work with them, they each also have identified an inner coach who helps them manage themselves more productively in conflict.

Clyde Dale: Clyde's gremlin is a smoldering volcano, a single piece of bad news away from erupting. It repeatedly tells him, "Here it goes again" and "You better straighten these people out." Clyde's inner coach is working hard to remind him to "stay curious."

Vic Tom: Vic has been a big Charlie Brown fan his whole life, so it should be no surprise that his gremlin sees him as an inevitable loser, just waiting to have the football pulled away as he is about to kick it. Charlie tells him, "You'll lose no matter what you do" and counsels him to accept his lot in life. This gremlin accounted for the way Vic dealt with many of the situations leading up to the quarterly management meeting. His behavior during the meeting was guided by a different gremlin, which played on his angry self-righteousness and urged him to attack. Vic's inner coach cheers him on with "You can make a difference" and "This can be sorted out."

Perry Noyd: Perry's gremlin brings to mind the L'il Abner comic strip character, Joe Bftsplk — the one with the black cloud over his head. Joe sees the dark lining in every silver cloud. In conflict, he warns Perry that "it will only get worse" and discourages him with "why bother?" Perry's inner coach encourages him: "This is worth sorting out. You can handle this."

Doug Right: Doug's drill sergeant gremlin drives both Doug and those around him to perfection. In conflict, it urges Doug to shoot first and ask questions later. It tells him, "You know best. They just don't get it." Doug's inner coach, however, coaxes him to slow down and say, "I wonder what their point of view is."

 *Dean Isle:* Dean's gremlin is a mole, which burrows for cover at the first sign of trouble. His mole pauses long enough to say, "It's probably your fault anyway" before sounding the alarm to "run away, run away." Dean's inner coach reminds him, "They're yelling for themselves, not at you" and encourages him to take a risk and confront problems.

Dinah Myte: Dinah has enjoyed a long relationship with her gremlin, Miss Should, a stern disciplinarian with a black and white view of the world. In conflict, Miss Should's judgments are the blinders that often prevent Dinah from seeing other perspectives. Miss Should is often heard saying, "How dare they?" and "That is just *wrong.*" Dinah's inner coach quietly suggests, "There are two sides to every story."

Melanie Low: Since childhood, Melanie has identified with Shirley Temple, who wants everyone to get along and believes that being nice to people will always be rewarded. In conflict, Shirley frets that someone might not like Melanie and warns her that "you better make them happy." Melanie's inner coach constantly reassures her that "it's okay if they don't like you for a little while" and that "you are not responsible for their feelings."

Lance Lott: Lance has always identified with Indiana Jones, who braves great odds in pursuit of justice. In conflict, Indiana spurs Lance into action and even provides an inspiring soundtrack to accompany his charge. It tells Lance, "You don't have to take this" and "Don't put up with that." Lance's inner coach reminds him to slow down and assess a situation because "it's not life-threatening; we can sort this out."

Gale Reasoner: Gale often hears the righteous voice of her gremlin, Wonder Woman, as she hurries to the rescue of those foolish people who "just don't get it." In conflict, Wonder Woman tells her, "You would never do something like that" and urges her to "get in there." Gale's inner coach proposes a softer approach because "we all make mistakes" and "they're doing the best they can."

Marko Blunt: Marko's gremlin is a sledgehammer, similar to the one that served him so well early in his working life. In conflict, it tells Marko that the only way to deal with a brick wall is to hammer home your point — again and again. His gremlin often says, "That's garbage" and "You know what's right." Marko's inner coach is planting the seed that there may be room for more than one perspective and that "everyone can have their point of view."

What to do about our gremlins

The beauty of Carson's book *Taming Your Gremlin* lies in its simplicity. He advises us to "simply notice" our gremlin. He warns us not to analyze or debate it, lest we end up like Br'er Rabbit — stuck fast to the tar baby. We'll never win an argument with it, and because it feeds off our attention, attempts to conquer it will serve only to strengthen it.

But when we "simply notice," we create separation. We become the observer, separate from what we observe. We are able to realize *we are not our gremlin*. It is a part of us, but not who we are. We can learn from it, for its warnings are attempts to protect an underlying value. Some people thank their gremlin for its opinion and then consider other perspectives and alternatives. Others use humor to create separation, giving their gremlins amusing names and personas ("George," the knuckle-dragging gorilla).

In conflict, we can "simply notice" our impulse — be it fight or flight. That momentary separation removes us, however fleetingly, from the drama triangle and allows us to choose our role and our approach. Even if we choose to respond angrily or to give in, we do so deliberately, not through habit or fear.

Listen to your inner coach

Just as our gremlins and their negative self-talk can trap us on the triangle, we can tap into an "inner coach" to support us to choose other roles. Our inner coach embodies positive and productive attitudes. It reminds us of the value of curiosity, empathy, and assertiveness, with statements such as:

"I can handle this."

"I wonder what's causing them to do that."

"I can make a difference."

"This isn't life-threatening."

"Stay curious — all behavior makes sense."

"I don't need to be perfect to have an opinion."

"It's okay if they don't like me for a little while."

"I'm not responsible for their feelings."

"This is worth sorting out."

"They're yelling at [the organization/uniform/company], not at me."

Some people relate more easily to an image than to an inner voice. One student visualized a "stop" sign, which served to buy him precious seconds at the base of anger mountain. Another visualized the angry energy as a river and himself as a rock around which the water flowed. Some people take the concept of a coach a step further by creating a *champion*. A colleague calls it "the angel on my shoulder." It draws forth her strength and wisdom. A champion can be a person or character who embodies the qualities you seek — courage, compassion, curiosity, or composure. Other people develop a personal mantra such as "Stay curious" or "You can handle this."

Have fun with it. Be creative. Do whatever it takes to give yourself the time and space to assess situations and choose the best response for you.

Summary

Knowing ourselves and our triggers allows us to develop a preventive maintenance program that can serve us when conflict surfaces.

Self-management begins with awareness of our body and breathing. The seemingly simple act of planting both feet on the ground and breathing deeply can empower us in times of stress and in the face of anger.

Our gremlins urge us to respond to conflict aggressively or passively, but not collaboratively. If we can avoid engaging our gremlins and instead simply observe them, we create separation and choice.

You also can create an inner coach to empower and support you in conflict. Your inner coach embodies positive and productive attitudes and will remind you of the value of curiosity, empathy, and assertiveness.

From theory to practice

To discover your fight gremlin, think of a time when you reacted aggressively to a situation in which you would have preferred to respond assertively. Jot down a few notes about the circumstances, your thoughts, and your feelings.

As you revisit the situation and the events that triggered you, ask yourself the following questions:
- What did you think?
- How did you feel?
- What were you telling yourself?
- What was your impulse?
- What did you do?

If your experience is mainly one of recalling the thoughts you had (or your "inner voice") ask yourself the following:
- What did the inner voice sound like?
- What did it say?
- What was the tone of voice?
- How loud/soft was it?

Give those thoughts (or that inner voice) a name.

If your experience is more visual, ask yourself the following:
- What does it sound like?
- What does it look like?
- Size, shape, color?
- How does it act?
- What does it tell you?

Then attach a name to that image. (You might consider an animal, object or character from a cartoon, fairy tale or movie.)

If your experience is mainly one of a feeling, ask yourself the following:
- Where in your body is the feeling the strongest?
- How strong is it?
- How would you describe the feeling?
- To what impulse does the feeling lead?

Then give the feeling a name.

Observe and acknowledge your gremlin. Ask yourself, in what situations does it get you into trouble? What self-talk do you associate with it? What actions result from your gremlin's narrative?

Finally, create an inner coach or champion for yourself. What more productive message would you like to send yourself when you are triggered or confronted by conflict? What image or voice or person might you associate with that message? How would you feel when you heard the message? You may even wish to give your coach or champion a name if that would help you draw on it in stressful times.

You may wish to repeat steps 1 to 5 above for your flight gremlin by considering a time when you remained passive but wished you had been more assertive.

CHAPTER 9

THE POWER OF LISTENING

> *Give everyone their "one minute."*
> — Danaan Parry, *Warriors of the Heart*

Though the journey through conflict may seem perilous, we each have available to us a power to ease our way. This power quells anger, builds bridges of understanding, and wins us a hearing with even the most stubborn person. It is freely accessible to us and requires only that we let go of the need to be right (although some might find this a steep price). This greatly underused power is that of listening.

One of my mentors, Danaan Parry, held a black belt in aikido and used aikido principles to teach conflict resolution. He noted that aikido practitioners referred to their opponent as their "partner" and when attacked would "step beside and walk with" the other person. From that position, they could divert the other person's energy without needing to meet it head-on. In conflict, we "walk with" another when we fully and openly listen to their story. This understanding allows us to redirect confrontational energy toward collaboration.

In her book *Fierce Conversations,* Susan Scott notes that the word "conversation" stems from the Latin "to speak with." She observes that many people prefer to have "versations," without the bother of having to listen to the other person. Listening is what puts the "con" in "conversation."

Force

The North Wind and the Sun

Aesop illustrated the power of empathy in his fable "The North Wind and the Sun," in which the title characters argued over who was more powerful. They agreed to have a contest: whoever could strip a traveler of his cloak would be the winner. The North Wind went first and blew with all his might, but the harder he blew the more closely the traveler wrapped his cloak around him. At last, the Wind gave up and invited the Sun to try. The Sun shone all his warmth on the traveler, who soon had no need to wear his cloak and slung it over his shoulder. Aesop used this fable to illustrate that persuasion is better than force.

In conflict, people often revert to the North Wind's approach and rely on force to make their point. When met by resistance, they speak more loudly and argue more vigorously, becoming "blowhards," so to speak. Such an onslaught, however, only causes the other person to cling more tightly to the "cloak" of their own perspective. The Sun's approach serves us better in these situations. We can reduce resistance by shining rays of attention and empathy on the other person. Once they feel heard and understood, they have less need to hang on to their position and a greater willingness to hear our perspective.

Why listen?

Despite Aesop's lesson, you might think to yourself, "Why the heck should I spend my precious time and energy listening to the boneheads I'm in conflict with? If they had any sense in the first place, they would have seen that I'm right and there wouldn't even be a conflict. If anyone should be listening, *they* should." And you may be right, although when both people adopt this approach there will be a whole lot of

Empathy

talking and very little listening going on. There are several benefits to adopting a listen first, talk second approach.

First of all, listening defuses anger in another person. You may have heard the saying that "they're not yelling at me, they're yelling for themselves." People in conflict often speak aggressively to ensure the other person understands the importance of the points they are trying to make. When we listen instead of reacting, the other person can tell their story without interruption. As they do so, they blow off steam and may even begin to see us differently. After all, villains are uncaring and controlling. When we demonstrate a contradictory quality, such as empathy, we encourage the other person to see us as someone they can work with.

Second, listening broadens our perspective on the problem. We can learn what motivates the other person, what underlies their resistance or frustration. New information may create previously unseen possibilities. There is a reason effective negotiators and salespeople do more listening than talking.

Finally, listening to another can win us a hearing from them. In some "conversations" one person talks until they have to pause for breath, which allows the other person to jump in and contradict them. The first person to breathe loses! People seldom will let go of their positions and consider a different perspective until they feel heard and understood. As Stephen Covey says, "Seek first to understand, then to be understood."

Confrontational conversations are like a game of ping-pong, marked by a series of "yes, buts" as one person immediately rebuts the other's points. An example is the meeting between Turm-Oil's manager of distribution, Doug Right, and systems technician Dean Isle over the computerized inventory system.

"This program has performed an illegal operation"

Dean nervously glances at the clock at the bottom of his computer screen as his ten o'clock meeting with Doug approaches. He reviews his notes again and wishes for the umpteenth time that he had installed a back door in his office. At 9:59, he hears Doug's booming voice down the hall.

"Yes, I *know* it's a problem, Big Bob. Yes, I *am* working on it. No, it *won't* happen again." Doug's frame fills the doorway. He snaps his cellphone shut and glares at a stiffening Dean.

He wastes no time. "Let's cut to the chase, Dean. This new computerized inventory system sucks." Doug plants himself in the chair in front of Dean's desk and leans forward, one hand on the desk. Dean remains motionless, staring at the "Star Wars" poster behind Doug. "Did you hear me? Your system is killing us."

"Your system is killing us."

Dean's eyes widen as he struggles for a reply. "I understand," he finally bleats.

"No, you don't understand. The software locks, orders have been delayed, and worst of all this so-called automatic inventory update doesn't update anything. If you understood, you would have fixed it by now."

Dean fidgets and mumbles, "It's not that bad. All systems have the odd glitch or two."

His attempt to downplay the problem only fuels Doug's anger. "Not that bad?! I live in the real world, Dean. I'm the one who has to deal with customers who've been shorted. The odd glitch?! Give me a break!"

Doug's attack sparks a retort from Dean. "You give *me* a break. The system is only as good as the operators, Doug."

"Yes, but you assured me in this very office that the system was user-friendly. You have a very twisted view of user-friendly."

"It worked fine when I tested it. You people must not be following the manual."

"You people must not be following the manual."

"If it was in English, we might have a fighting chance. It's so filled with technobabble that it's worthless."

"Worthless? I spent weeks making sure it was accurate."

"Well, you should have spent that time fixing the system."

"Look, I don't have time to hold your hand because you can't handle technology. You warehouse guys complain any time we change anything. You give it a half-hearted effort, then blame some-one else."

Both men are now sitting tall and leaning forward as their voices rise. Neither waits for the other to finish before contradicting him. "Change is fine," Doug spits through his clenched jaw, "as long as it makes things better. This has been a disaster from Day 1."

"The system would make things better if you gave it a fair shot."

"We have — and it's been a waste of time. Are you going to fix this or what?"

"Okay, okay, just back off for a minute." Dean's fingers dart around the keyboard and he seems to relax slightly while dealing with his computer rather than his angry colleague. He shakes his head and rolls his eyes. "Look at this," he says, smugly pointing to the screen. "One of your guys turned off the auto-update feature. No wonder it didn't update the inventory. There — I've switched it back on. Jeez, just read the manual and the system will be fine."

Doug is far from happy. He glares at Dean, his finger now inch-es from Dean's nose. "Look, the auto-update is just the tip of the iceberg. Any more problems with this joke you call a system and I'll be telling Clyde to get someone in here who knows what they're doing." He pushes his chair back noisily and strides from Dean's office without looking back.

DEBATE, NOT DIALOGUE

In this discussion, Dean and Doug engaged in a classic statement-reaction debate. More intent on talking than listening, they attacked, rebutted, denied, and defended. Tempers rose; understanding evap-orated. The problem persisted and their relationship soured. Not exactly a good day at the office for either of them. Doug left the meeting intent on gathering enough ammunition to demand that Clyde replace Dean. Dean left more concerned with defending himself than with supporting Doug.

Doug and Dean share responsibility for the failed communication during the meeting, and either one of them could have broken the chain reaction of defensiveness. Let's examine Dean's contribution. Despite having read three books on communication and conflict resolution, Dean failed, when under pressure, to put theory into practice. His conflict gremlins led him into some classic communication pitfalls as he:

- interrupted Doug
- minimized Doug's concerns ("It's not that bad")
- deflected responsibility ("The system is only as good as the operators")
- blamed and assumed ("You people must not be following the manual")
- generalized ("You guys complain any time we change anything")

These reactions obscured valid points on both sides. They blocked collaboration even though Doug and Dean had a mutual interest in improving the system. Their conversation degenerated into a ping-pong game of attack and defend. Had Dean really listened, he could have changed the game and produced a far more satisfying outcome.

Silence *is* golden

Dean could have begun by allowing and encouraging Doug to tell his story — without interruption, without editorials. Granted, listening intently is a challenge even in a regular conversation and more so when the other person's story paints us as the villain. Our urge to fight or flee leads us to defend and justify ourselves or to withdraw. Either way, we are not listening.

My friend Danaan Parry taught the simple concept of "giving people their one minute" to emphasize the importance of listening.

(When I mentioned this to one group of students, one of the cheekier participants asked, "So if I shut up for one minute, then I can yell at them?") To clarify, "giving someone their one minute" means listening with genuine curiosity and requires us to temporarily put our story aside. This simple but challenging concept can pay immediate dividends in conflict.

Instead of becoming defensive, Dean could have taken a breath, made eye contact, and nodded as Doug vented his concerns.

Proving you understand

Although silence serves as a foundation for understanding, at some point the other person will require evidence that their message has been received. Yet even though people want to be heard, few expect unconditional agreement. In the 1970s, communication experts counseled people to demonstrate understanding with the phrase "What I hear you saying is ..." Unfortunately, people have since shortened this to "I hear you" or "I understand." These phrases have become so trite that they are as likely to inflame the other person as to reassure them. Depending on the context and delivery, they often interpret such expressions as "Yeah, yeah, shut up, it's my turn to talk." People in conflict assume we *don't* understand them — until we demonstrate otherwise.

We can take comfort, however, in knowing we don't have to be "right" in demonstrating our understanding. As long as we are genuine in our attempt, the other person will help us. After all, they *want* us to understand. They will clarify any points we may have missed or misunderstood. As they sense our interest and begin to feel respected, they normally relax and expand on their points less aggressively. This not only calms the tone of the conversation but also uncovers valuable information.

Dean responded to Doug's initial outburst by assuring him, "I understand." Maybe he did, maybe he didn't. But in Doug's mind the response was so generic and unconvincing that it simply reinforced his view that Dean clearly *didn't* understand anything. To change Doug's perception of him as the uncaring villain, Dean needed to demonstrate that he understood. To twist Don Quixote's phrase, the proof of the pudding is in the paraphrasing.

How to get the full story

Remember the three elements of conflict stories presented in Chapter 3: the plot, the characters, and the theme or conflict. These elements can guide us to listen at increasingly deep levels for the facts, the feelings, and the unmet needs — to listen for the full story.

FOLLOW THE PLOT

The plot provides the framework of the story — how events unfolded, what was said and done. We often can put the facts and details we hear together with our own knowledge to create a fuller understanding of the situation. If we can at least agree on the events and how they unfolded, we have the foundation for a common story in which we can explore differences. Sometimes one new piece of information can clarify an assumption and shed new light on a conflict.

We can confirm our understanding of another by *paraphrasing* them — restating their story in our own words. This does not mean parroting them, however, as this usually will be seen as patronizing or manipulative. By rephrasing their words, we offer the speaker an opportunity to clarify details or add any important points.

UNDERSTAND THE "CHARACTER" — FEELINGS AND MOTIVATION

The facts constitute only the outer layer of a conflict story. Feelings and motivation provide a context for what was said and done. Why are these events important to the person? What motivated them to act as they did? How were they feeling at the time? None of this will be readily apparent, yet until we discover "when the knife went in," we have little hope of understanding the conflict.

Exploring feelings and motivations sounds simple in theory but can be challenging and a bit scary in practice. We often shy away from the anger and frustration in a person's conflict story. We are conditioned at an early age to avoid such emotions. To empathize with another person, we must make a conscious effort to overcome that conditioning.

In our example, Dean clearly was uncomfortable with Doug's anger. Accordingly, he tried to downplay Doug's frustration with the inventory control system and minimize the problems Doug faced. Unfortunately, but predictably, his approach backfired. Dean's apparent lack of understanding added insult to injury for Doug and stoked the very anger Dean was attempting to avoid.

FOCUS ON UNMET NEEDS

As discussed in Chapter 1, we can expect the stories of those with whom we are in conflict to paint them as the victim and us as the villain. These stories focus on past wrongs and are characterized by blame and personal attacks. This narrow lens blinds people to new possibilities and perspectives.

We can open avenues for resolution by offering the other person a new lens through which to view the conflict. In their story, buried amidst the anger, accusations, and hurt, lie unmet needs — the source of their "wound." These unmet needs hold the key to resolving the conflict, for they cause the other person to view us as the villain. Villains deprive people of what they hold dear and stand between them and happiness. If we can clarify their unmet needs, we can support them to move beyond the drama triangle to focus on solving the problem.

To listen deeply is challenging, for even the other person might not be aware of what they need. They likely are so caught up in their reaction to the conflict that they are unable to see beyond the drama. They just know that they are upset and see us as to blame. To avoid reacting to this blame and to stay focused on their unmet need require patience and curiosity on our part. One way to maintain this curiosity is to ask ourselves, "What important need do they have that is unfulfilled?" or "What do they lack or fear that drives them to see us as the villain?" They will be more than happy to tell us what they *don't* want. We can help move the situation forward by focusing them on what they *do* want.

"THIS PROGRAM HAS PERFORMED AN ILLEGAL OPERATION" — REBOOTED

How might the conversation have gone if Dean had been able to steel himself and remain grounded in the face of Doug's anger?

As Doug's frame fills the doorway, Dean draws a deep breath and stands up. He motions Doug to take a seat. "Thanks for coming by, Doug. I know things haven't been going well with the new inventory control system."

Doug wastes no time. "That's an understatement. It's a joke."

Dean leans forward. "What's going on with it?"

"The software locks, orders have been delayed, and worst of all this so-called automatic inventory update doesn't update anything."

"Ouch. That sounds worse than I thought."

"Now you're getting it, Dean. You try dealing with Big Bob when we've run out of his precious Banana Blend. He's on me like ugly on an ape."

Dean winces. "So, basically, the system isn't working and you're the one left holding the bag with the customers."

"You're the one left holding the bag with the customers."

Doug sags in his chair and shakes his head as he recalls his most recent phone call from Big Bob. He sighs and spreads his palms upward in resignation. "You told me the new system would be user-friendly and eliminate mistakes like this. It's causing more problems than it's solving."

Dean pauses and reflects. "Okay. Let me make sure I've got the picture. It locks. It doesn't flag inventory shortages. And you're taking heat about it from the customers."

"That's it in a nutshell. We've got to get a handle on this — and soon."

Dean sits back and glances at his notes. "I agree. Help me out for a minute because I don't understand what could have happened.

When I tested the system, it operated within expected parameters, including the automatic updating feature. And I double-checked the operating manual you asked for. Something isn't adding up, so let's go over this again. When does it lock up?"

Within minutes, Doug and Dean isolate the problem that causes the system to lock up. They discover that Marko and Lance find it difficult to learn from an operating manual and need more hands-on training. Dean says he will be happy to spend some time with them. Dean also says he can tweak the system to eliminate the lock-ups. Doug actually thanks Dean before bustling off to fight yet another fire. Dean reflects for a moment and realizes that the meeting went a lot better than he could have imagined.

In this scenario, Dean listened to Doug's story at three levels. He captured the facts about the system malfunctions, he empathized with Doug's frustration and embarrassment in dealing with customers, and he pinpointed Doug's need for reliability and support. This understanding laid a foundation for cooperation and uncovered new possibilities for resolution.

A metaphor is worth a thousand words

Conflict stirs many feelings and thoughts. We often find it a challenge to identify and express all that might be going on for us. Sometimes we cannot find words to capture complex emotional experiences. Metaphors can help. Because they are not literal, they connect us with our listener at an emotional level, planting the seeds of empathy.

Metaphors weave their way through most conversations. ("I'm between a rock and a hard place here.") The images associated with a metaphor move a conversation to a deeper level and provide clues to both feelings and underlying needs. People who are reluctant to reveal how hurt or overwhelmed they feel may be more comfortable expressing their situation as "a slap in the face" or being "a fish out of water" in a new job. These images provide clues to the other person's unmet needs and can guide us to a deeper understanding of their story.

As listeners, we can introduce metaphors to check out how accurately we have understood a speaker. ("So your department knows where it's supposed to go but doesn't have a road map.") Even if we don't have it quite right, the other person often will build on the metaphor to clarify their point. ("It's not that we don't have a road map; we don't have any gas for our car.") A colleague once described how frustrated she felt working under a new boss whose style and vision differed from her own. "Sounds like you're really not on the same page," I reflected. She smiled. "We're not even in the same library." The imagery spoke "volumes" and left no doubt about how disconnected she felt. By providing everyday imagery, metaphors allow us to — if you'll excuse another one — begin to weave the threads of our separate stories into the fabric of collaboration.

The importance of being genuine

To prevent us from being manipulated, we have all been issued, at birth, a BS detector. It becomes finely tuned through experience. It is the gut feeling we get when someone or something doesn't quite ring true. Conversely, it signals us when other people can be trusted. It instinctively lets us know if someone is simply saying the right thing or is giving us the straight goods.

Though not officially studying the BS detector, a celebrated study at UCLA found that, in face-to-face communication, only seven percent of the overall message was conveyed by the words. The majority of the communication occurred through tone of voice, facial expressions, and body language. Sarcasm is a prime example: the tone, not the words, causes the knife to go in. When we receive mixed messages, our built-in BS detector ignores the words and tunes in to the nonverbal communication. Sincerity and genuineness are at the heart of good listening. For this reason, use words and expressions that come naturally to you, as demonstrated by the following story.

During a workshop many years ago I introduced "active listening." We discussed the danger of a listener's response seeming scripted and manipulative. As practice, I asked participants to respond to me as if I were a co-worker talking to them over coffee on a Monday morning. I ranted, "I can't believe it! I spent all weekend working on this stupid presentation and they canceled it — no notice!" Their responses ranged from "That must be really irritating" to "You sound pretty ticked off about wasting your weekend." One young woman, sporting a punk look with bright pink hair and piercings, slouched in her chair, looked me in the eye, shook her head, and uttered the single word: "Pisser!" When I finally stopped laughing, I had to admit that I felt *heard*.

Being real is more important than being precise. Find ways to bring who you are to the conversation. Though the emotion that accompanies conflict is stressful, it also provides an opportunity to build deeper relationships with the other person. When we resolve a conflict, we experience both satisfaction and connection. Therein lies the joy of conflict resolution.

Summary

Give everyone their "one minute." People are unlikely to listen to you until they feel you've listened to them.

Listen for their full story: facts, feelings, and unmet needs. At the heart of every conflict story lie unmet needs.

Prove you are listening by reflecting your understanding back to them.

Being genuine is more important than being precise.

From theory to practice

In conversations, listen specifically for each of the following. Focus on each for a week or rotate them through the week:

- facts (the plot of their story)
- feelings (whether expressed directly or not)
- unmet needs (what does the person value, but lack?)

Listen for metaphors other people use. Look for opportunities to use metaphors either to summarize their experience or to describe your own.

Consider the feelings and unmet needs associated with each of the following metaphors. The first one has been completed as an example.

METAPHOR	FEELING	UNMET NEED
end of my rope	overwhelmed, demoralized	support
out of the loop		
see me as the heavy		
between a rock and a hard place		
blindsided or ambushed		
flying by the seat of my pants		
hitting a wall		
he's a lone wolf		
out on a limb		
hung out to dry		

CHAPTER 10

Spinning the Straw of Defensiveness

Within resistance lie unmet needs.

In the fairy tale "Rumpelstiltskin," the title character helps a poor miller's daughter accomplish the seemingly impossible task of spinning straw into gold. Because she appears to be able to create something valuable from something so common, she wins the king's hand and, after a few adventures, lives happily ever after. The straw in that story is like defensiveness in conflict — commonplace and seen to have little value. Yet with empathy and curiosity, it too can be spun into something valuable: the gold of understanding.

We can begin by looking at defensiveness as a behavior rather than a personality flaw. When people behave defensively, they are sending us a message. If we remain curious, we can begin to understand the message and, in turn, the person. This understanding is the foundation for resolution.

The chain reaction of defensiveness

Defensiveness, in some form, surfaces in virtually every conflict. Often one person's defensive response will trigger the other person, setting off a chain reaction in which each person feels "hit" first.

The Turm-Oil quarterly meeting is a classic example. Vic felt unfairly blamed by Clyde for the drop in sales and deflected the discussion to what he saw as a lack of support. His response triggered Perry, who justified his decision ("I'm not Santa Claus, you know") and denied the budget was the real problem. This denial infuriated Vic even more and he built his case further when he blamed Doug and the shipping department for customer dissatisfaction. Doug in turn deflected the attack to Dean and the problems with the inventory control software. Dean froze (likely hoping the conflict would pass him by if he kept quiet and blended in with the foliage). Vic criticized Dinah because she didn't have brochures ready for a trade show; she, in turn, blamed Vic for his lack of communication about the brochures. We can see that each defensive response prompted a similar reaction from another person.

This chain reaction locks us firmly on the drama triangle as we protest our innocence and defend our good name. Clearly *we* are being unfairly labeled as the villain when, in fact, *they* are the villain, for who but a villain would treat us so unfairly and maliciously?

Defining defensiveness

A dear friend and valued colleague, Donna Soules, chose defensiveness as her thesis topic for a master's degree in conflict resolution. With the promise of free food and a rustic setting, she enlisted a dozen practicing mediators as her focus group. They created a working definition of defensiveness as "a behavioral response to a perceived threat or attack, often to one's self-esteem or well-being." Donna's thesis examines defensiveness as a "negotiation of face" and cites Freud's reference to an "anxiety about an unbearable idea." Consider situations in which you perceive yourself judged to be a villain — a bad parent, disloyal team member, or incompetent worker. For most of us, the idea of being the villain is an unbearable one. For example, if I miss a deadline and you call me "unprofessional," I could agree that my assignment was late, but would bristle at the attack on my character. I would experience you as overreacting and generalizing — "removing the fly from my face with a hatchet," in the words of an old Chinese proverb. Our subsequent conversation would involve my "negotiation of face."

But we should not confuse defensiveness with assertiveness. Defensive behavior attacks the other person or negates their point of view. Assertive behavior, as discussed in Chapter 13, sets limits on how we let others treat us. It allows room for the other person's opinions and concerns, provided they are delivered respectfully. Defensiveness focuses on the content of another person's message, assertiveness on how that message is delivered.

Spinning the gold of understanding

When I was learning to mediate, I assumed that my job was to eliminate emotion from the conversation. If we could all be calm and rational, I reasoned, we would resolve the situation more effectively and efficiently. I soon realized that emotions not only were a natural part of conflict but also could guide me to the source of the conflict. Emotions need to be managed, not quashed. Once I became more comfortable with emotions (or at least more comfortable with my discomfort in the face of them), I began to view anger and frustration as symptoms of deeper, unmet needs. Until those needs were identified and addressed, any solution would be superficial and the root conflict ultimately would resurface in another form.

Over time, I developed a mental image to remind me to be curious in the face of defensiveness: I visualize a "dig here" sign. This helps me manage my impulse to revert to judgment or counterattack. Instead, I'm (usually) able to step back and ask myself, "What's going on for them right now? In what ways are they feeling attacked?" By remaining curious, I allow and encourage the other person to tell their side of the story, explain their concerns, and clarify their intentions. Once we are able to listen to someone's story without feeling the need to make it conform to our own view, we open the doors to invaluable understanding.

Forms of defensiveness: more lessons from the sandbox

Chapter 2 introduced two basic conflict dynamics: our resistance to being cast as the villain and our desire to proclaim our innocence as the victim. Here are some defensive behaviors you likely have encountered (and, of course, never used yourself), along with some strategies for dealing with them.

THEY HIT ME FIRST (JUSTIFICATION)

This is one of the more impulsive defensive reactions. It's shorthand for "Once you understand the entire story, you'll see that I was wronged first and that I pursue justice, as a good hero does." This type of reaction indicates the person feels misunderstood or unheard. They need a chance to tell their side of the story and provide a context for their actions. (This strategy does not excuse bad behavior but does help us understand and deal with it.)

FIGURE 10A
JUSTIFICATION

When confronted with "they hit me first," step back, hear the person out, then show them you understand their perspective. People usually will acknowledge their role in a conflict if they can do so without losing face or being judged as a villain. You can acknowledge their intent, yet still confront problem behavior.

I DIDN'T DO IT (DENIAL)

Picture a child, mouth covered with chocolate sauce, caught red-handed (or chocolate-mouthed) as Mom suddenly enters the room. Knowing he's in for it now, he instinctively blurts, "I didn't do anything." As adults, we have developed slightly more sophisticated but equally impulsive versions of denial, such as "It's not my fault. The guys in shipping screwed up."

This type of defensive reaction speaks less to the specifics of an incident than to a general declaration that "I'm not a villain." We fear the "unbearable idea" that we're a bad person just because we made a mis-

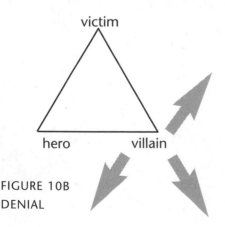

FIGURE 10B
DENIAL

take. When confronted with this defensive reaction, remember it is driven by fear. Seek to reassure the other person that they can safely engage in an open and honest discussion of the situation. We can reassure them by focusing on the future rather than dwelling on the past. We also can emphasize the mutual benefit of exploring and resolving the situation.

ALL THE OTHER KIDS DO IT (DEFLECTION)

The adult version of this familiar line occurs when an employee's extended lunch break is questioned by a supervisor. When other excuses failed, we likely would hear, "Why are you picking on me? Everyone else takes long lunches!"

FIGURE 10C
DEFLECTION

This reaction says, "I'm not a villain. Everyone does this. I'm actually a victim because you're singling me out." When confronted with a deflection, don't get sidetracked. Acknowledge the person's point if it's relevant, while continuing to focus on the original problem.

YOUR MOMMA WEARS ARMY BOOTS (BLAME AND COUNTERATTACK)

This approach exemplifies the adage that "the best defense is a good offense." It may involve the accusation "You're a fine one to talk. You're always late yourself." Or it may take the form of a counterattack on an unrelated issue. In defending themselves, the other person attempts to cast us as the real villain so that role doesn't fall to them. The unspoken message is: "You're worse than I am. You're not the hero. *You're* the villain."

FIGURE 10D
COUNTERATTACK

When confronted with a counterattack, resist the impulse to return fire or defend yourself, for this only creates a chain reaction of defensiveness. Instead, acknowledge the other person's perspective and perhaps agree to discuss their issues separately. If we lose our focus, the other person will have succeeded in their efforts to divert attention from our original issue.

I CAN'T HEAR YOU (WITHDRAWAL)

A child sits with her hands covering her ears, chanting loudly to herself, "I can't hear you." Teenagers, with the help of headphones and portable computer games, have refined this technique to include the laconic "whatever." Adult versions include simply walking away or clamming up. This avoidance of confrontation often is driven by a fear of conflict in general and, more specifically, a belief that if they engage, they will be seen as the villain. They are essentially saying, "If I don't play, I won't lose."

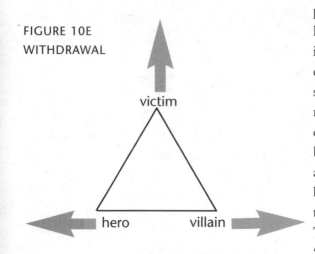

FIGURE 10E
WITHDRAWAL

When confronted with this defensive behavior, try to create a safe space to discuss the issue. Emphasize your desire to solve a problem, not attack them personally. Let the other person know what is at stake and why you see it as important to address the problem. We need to draw on our patience and persistence to build enough trust for the other person to engage with us.

Warming the climate

Defensive behavior increases with the level of judgment, hostility, and suspicion people experience. In a hostile climate, we are fully alert and ready to fend off perceived attacks on our character or well-being. We naturally view the other person as the villain against whose threats we must guard ourselves. The other person also responds to the tension, sensitive to their own need to defend themselves against us.

Consider how Clyde opened Turm-Oil's quarterly meeting on the topic of the sales figures. "Let's get on with this," he growled and drew a spreadsheet from his briefcase. "I won't beat around the bush. The numbers for the first quarter stink. We're hurting and, frankly, if you don't turn things around, there'll be some changes around here."

"If you don't turn things around, there'll be some changes around here."

His growls, judgment, and implied threat immediately created a tense atmosphere that understandably led Vic to defend his professional reputation and attempt to save face. Although defensiveness may surface as a specific reaction, it usually is the product of a hostile climate. To reduce defensiveness, we must not only treat the symptom but also "warm" the climate that fosters it. By remaining curious and empathetic, we encourage the other person to tell their story without fear of attack or judgment. When a person feels their perspective will be respected, suspicion thaws and trust builds.

Here's how Clyde might have opened the meeting to set a more supportive climate — devoid of the judgment, hostility, and suspicion that marked the earlier example. He could have said, "Folks, I just received the sales figures for the first quarter and they aren't pretty. I know it's been a stressful couple of months for everyone, and today I want us to put our heads together and figure out how to turn this around." He could have acknowledged that it's been rough for Vic on the front lines and invited him to talk about his challenges. Vic would have felt less need to defend himself and would likely have provided valuable insight into the issues the company needed to address to move forward.

Doug separates the person from the problem

In Chapter 9, we eavesdropped on a meeting between Doug and Dean over the inventory control software. In that meeting, both of them quickly fell into a chain reaction of defensiveness. We looked at how Dean could have used the power of listening to defuse Doug's anger, understand the problem, and develop a strategy to move forward. Let's reverse the roles and see how Doug could have created a more supportive, less confrontational climate to reduce Dean's defensiveness and build understanding and cooperation.

Doug Right's massive frame fills the doorway of Dean Isle's small office. He pauses until Dean looks up. "Got a few minutes to work with me on this crazy inventory system?" Dean fidgets one last time with his keyboard, reluctantly invites Doug to sit down, and mumbles, "It's not that bad. All systems have the odd glitch or two."

Doug bites back his impulse to refute Dean's attempt to downplay the problems. "I expected the odd wrinkle, Dean, but we've been struggling with this system for weeks now. My guys are at the end of their rope and the customers are not happy."

"Give me a break, Doug. It worked fine when I tested it. You people must not be following the manual. The system is only as good as the operators."

"The system is only as good as the operators."

Doug takes a deep breath and resists his urge to tell Dean what he can do with his manual. "That may well be, Dean. I know you've been working hard to get this thing up and running. I'm hoping we can put our heads together for a few minutes and come up with a plan to deal with these glitches."

"The system is fine — and I spent weeks making sure the manual was idiot-proof."

"Whoa, Dean. Cool it with the idiot-proof stuff. Let's stick to the issue here. We're doing the best we can with the manual, and yet there are still things going on that we can't sort out. We need your expertise here."

Despite some lingering wariness, Dean seems to relax. "That's fine, just so long as everyone doesn't try to hang this on me. The system will work."

"That's great, Dean. I hoped we could start by looking at the details of a couple of problems we encountered last week."

"We need your expertise here."

In this conversation, Doug did several things to reduce Dean's defensiveness and encourage his cooperation. Most important (and for him, most difficult), he was able to control his impulses to counterattack when Dean minimized the problem and blamed the shipping department for failing to follow the manual. Instead, Doug warmed the climate by expressing his desire to work with Dean and acknowledging Dean's efforts and expertise. This approach reduced Dean's anxiety about the "unbearable idea" that he was incompetent or even would lose his job. And finally, Doug kept refocusing on his specific concerns with the system. Over time, Dean no longer felt the need to defend himself and was willing to work with Doug to examine the problem.

In the earlier version of this conversation, Doug's goal was to show he was right. The resulting defensiveness prevented any meaningful discussion. In the second version, he successfully focused on obtaining Dean's help and solving the problem. The defensiveness evaporated in the warmer atmosphere Doug created.

When you hit bedrock

Sometimes a person's defensive behavior is so deeply rooted in repressed anger, grief, or fear that we may be unable to reduce or manage it. In such cases, the best we can do is acknowledge their reaction and express our desire to work with them. If they spurn our efforts to collaborate, we can work with our own conflict gremlins to ensure we don't take the defensiveness personally, then explore ways to get what we need without their cooperation.

Summary

Defensiveness can be defined as "a behavioral response to a perceived threat or attack, often to one's self-esteem or well-being." It involves a negotiation of reputation and may reflect a person's anxiety about an "unbearable idea."

Two basic conflict dynamics define defensiveness: our resistance to being cast as the villain and our desire to proclaim our innocence as the victim.

When we view anger and frustration as symptoms of deeper, unmet needs, we can spin the gold of understanding by discovering what lies beneath defensive behavior. When you experience defensiveness in another person, treat it as an opportunity to "dig here" for their story.

Defensive behavior tends to arise in an atmosphere of judgment, hostility, and suspicion. By creating a supportive environment, we significantly reduce defensiveness.

From theory to practice

Identify one of your own defensive behaviors and the context in which you tend to exhibit it. What "unbearable idea" underlies your defensiveness?

Consider someone you experience as defensive. How do they exhibit their defensiveness? What "unbearable idea" might underlie their defensiveness? What one thing could you do to reduce their defensiveness?

CHAPTER 11

Escaping the Trap of Positions

A position is a short version of a longer story.

People in conflict often see themselves as having the "right" answer. When others disagree, confrontation ensues. Let's return to Turm-Oil's quarterly meeting, when the group was told that Vic Tom would be working from the main office. Each person who might be impacted by Vic's relocation had their solution to the problem. These positions could be summarized as "not in my backyard."

No room at the inn for Vic

Dinah, reluctantly accepting that Vic will be somewhere on the premises, sighs and shrugs. "Let's just put him next to Melanie. There's some room up there."

Melanie, not anxious to have Vic in her workspace, retorts, "No, there's not! All you have to do is move some of your stuff from the photocopy area and Vic could use that space."

Doug jumps in. "You're not moving any more junk back into the warehouse."

Clyde's eyes widen and he shakes his head in disgust as he listens to his staff

"All you have to do is move some of your stuff."

"You're not moving any more junk back into the warehouse."

bandy their positions. Finally, he sighs deeply and blurts, "Okay, then, I'll decide. Vic will use the boardroom. Case closed."

Those involved in the decision each declared their position — their solution, their demand. This set off a chain reaction in which people justified their own views and minimized and discredited those of their adversaries. Emotions built and discussion gave way to confrontation, as commonly happens when people focus on positions in a conflict.

Trapped by positions

A position can be defined as a person's desired solution in conflict, not necessarily taking other people into account, and often is accompanied by an attitude described by Danaan Parry in his book *Warriors of the Heart*:

> A strongly held belief, opinion, or attitude as to "how it is" or "how it should be." An expectation that there is only one way, one right outcome, one correct solution. A belief that truth is absolute and that you are the holder of that truth.

Positions reflect an attitude of certainty as to "what is right." They usually are preceded by words such as "I want," "We should," and "I won't." This language reveals an inflexible attitude and leads to the moral certainty and righteousness synonymous with the hero role.

Here are some examples of positions you might hear at work:

- I don't want to answer the phones at lunch
- That's not my responsibility
- We don't give cash refunds
- You must start work at 9:00
- I want a raise
- I don't want to work with ...

People also take positions in their personal lives:
- I should be able to stay out later than midnight
- No way I'm going to Hawaii for our holidays
- We should sell this place and buy a condo
- I want a cellphone
- You shouldn't golf both days this weekend

I'll leave it to you to guess which of these positions you'd be more likely to hear from a spouse than from a teenager.

When confronted by another's position, we tend to respond in kind, determinedly justifying and defending our own position. This power struggle focuses on winning and losing rather than on solving a problem. The confrontation may end with a grudging compromise. Unless the compromise meets the primary needs of each person, it is likely to be at best a stopgap measure in which each person focuses more on what they have given up than on what they have gained.

Of course, we're each going to have our preferred scenarios and proposed solutions when we enter conflict. Clinging to these positions, however, is what traps us on the drama triangle and leads us to cast the other person as an adversary. Luckily, there is a way to move beyond positional confrontation and create opportunities to collaborate.

Naming the topic

We can begin to shift the focus of conflict away from positions by identifying the topic of the conflict. Ask yourself, "In neutral and objective terms, what do we need to discuss and resolve?"

Consider the difference between the positional "I want to go to Hawaii" and the more neutral "I'd like to talk about our upcoming vacation." The position shuts down dialogue; the topic invites it. Dialogue allows for more than one perspective and creates room for everyone's story.

Clyde might have opened the discussion about Vic's move by saying, "I want to talk about our office space today and what we can do to accommodate Vic. Each of you will have a chance to let us know what you need. Then we'll look at some options that would work for everyone." He would have defused much of the confrontation triggered by people digging in on their positions.

Some common issues arising in organizational conflict include the following:

workload distribution	vacations
quality of work	management style
deadlines	scheduling
priorities	salaries and remuneration
roles and responsibilities	safety
resources	policies and procedures
communication	space

At home, conflict might arise around the following topics:

chores	curfew
toys and possessions	meals
roles and responsibilities	communication
homework	space
vacation	lifestyle (including tattoos
parenting styles	and body piercing)
condition of bedroom	

Notice that these lists avoid the use of loaded words that might trigger defensiveness ("*improved* quality of work" or "your *messy* bedroom"). Anything involving a number is more likely to be a demand than the introduction of a topic for discussion. "I'd like to talk to you about curfew" will get you further than "I'd like to talk to you about being in by midnight."

Identifying the problem in terms of a topic to be discussed or an issue to be resolved is a good first step in setting a collaborative tone and avoiding positional confrontation. Neutral topics set the stage to explore interests and needs.

The key to collaboration — interests and needs

At the heart of collaborative conflict resolution lie interests and needs. Chapter 3 outlined Abraham Maslow's belief that human beings are driven by fundamental needs. These needs motivate us — and trigger defensiveness when we feel them threatened. They lead us to adopt positions as a way to meet our needs.

Sometimes we take a position consciously; other times we react emotionally and impulsively. When we do the latter, we may take a position that ultimately does not serve our needs. For instance, a manager might eliminate flextime in an effort to increase productivity yet find that the resulting decline in morale decreases productivity instead. A valid need; an unproductive means to achieve it. Similarly, an employee who wasn't given an opportunity to speak at a staff meeting might boycott future meetings in protest. The position "I won't go" is unlikely to meet that person's need to provide meaningful input.

In their book *Getting to Yes,* Roger Fisher and Bill Ury relate a story of two sisters fighting over an orange. When a stalemate developed, they agreed to cut the orange in half — a fair solution, to be sure. One took her half, peeled it, and ate the fruit. The other also peeled her half, but used the peel to make marmalade and threw the fruit away. Each had assumed she knew why the other wanted the orange. Neither explained to the other why she wanted it. In the end, the compromise solution got each of them half of what was available, all because they focused on what they wanted (positions), not why they wanted it (interests and needs).

A positional approach results in either/or thinking and blinds people to other possibilities. Our energy goes into being right or proving the other person wrong. When we frame our conflict in terms of interests and needs, however, we create new opportunities for resolution. This focus fosters creativity and may lead to workable solutions that neither person had previously considered.

Shifting from positions to interests

When we are confronted by another person's position in a conflict, we can think of it as a "means to an end." Curiosity can help us overcome the impulse to attack and defend and can encourage us to seek to understand the "end." What is the other person attempting to achieve when they adopt their position? Similarly, when we find *ourselves* adopting a position in a conflict, we might take a breath and ask ourselves what we're hoping to achieve by that position. By asserting our interests rather than our position, we create less resistance and encourage flexibility.

A simple way to shift from positions to interests is to add the word "because" at the end of a positional statement. This word induces curiosity and leads us to ask questions about the reasons that drive a position. For example, the position "I want the corner office" when followed by "because" may lead to the interest "I need enough room to meet with clients."

Here's what might have happened if Gale Reasoner had been able to attend Turm-Oil's quarterly meeting. As the only telecommuter in the office, she would have had little at stake and been able to remain curious and objective when others argued their positions. To recap, Dinah told Clyde to locate Vic next to Melanie, prompting Melanie to counter that Vic should move into the photocopy area next to Dinah. Then Doug bristled at the mere possibility that anything more might go into the warehouse.

NO ROOM AT THE INN (REVISITED)

Gale looks a bit surprised at how quickly Dinah has "solved" the problem. "Why next to Melanie, Dinah?" she asks.

"Well," says Dinah, "there's no way I'm giving up my photocopy area. We went through this a year ago. Not only did it take up half my office, but people were always coming in and disturbing me when they wanted to use the photocopier."

"Why next to Melanie, Dinah?"

"So, however we sort this out, you need your privacy and adequate space in your office."

"Darn right I do. And I'm not going to traipse all the way back to the warehouse just to get some supplies or make a copy."

"Sounds like that would be a hassle," Gale acknowledges.

Dinah seems to relax a bit. "I need to be able to get things quick-ly. Sometimes people are waiting on the phone while I get an infor-mation pamphlet."

"So you need supplies somewhere in the general area of your office — easy to access."

"Yes. Is that too much to ask?"

Gale shrugs and shakes her head. "No, that doesn't seem unrea-sonable." She then turns to Melanie. "Melanie, you seemed pretty adamant you don't want Vic up front. How come?"

"Well," Melanie fidgets and looks at Vic's empty chair before continuing. "It's just that he's so ... loud. I have to concentrate on the phone calls and my data entry. It will give me a headache. Plus, two people would really make it cramped up front."

"So you want it quiet enough to be able to concentrate. And you need some elbow room."

Melanie reddens and looks down, seemingly embarrassed about being seen as demanding. "It's not like there's a lot of room up there to begin with."

Ever since the mention of the warehouse, Doug has been look-ing for an opportunity to jump in. "Whatever might happen out front, I just want to be clear that there's no way anything more is coming back into the warehouse," he pronounces. He leans for-ward and looks around, daring anyone to challenge him on the point.

Gale shifts in her chair and focuses her attention on the burly dis-tribution manager. "No one has decided anything yet about moving things back to the warehouse, Doug. But clearly that's a concern for you. In what way?"

Doug, warming to one of his pet peeves, needs little prodding. "First, the floor is covered with products. We're continually shuf-fling pallets when we have multiple orders. It's inefficient. Then you guys give us grief about it being cluttered and looking unprofes-sional when you bring customers back to look at the samples. I wish you would just leave us alone and let us do our job."

"Sounds like it's already cramped back there."

"Finally somebody gets the message."

"Loud and clear," says Gale. "You want to reduce the clutter so you can get at the orders efficiently. And the less foot traffic back there, the better."

"You get me that, Gale, and I'll be one happy camper."

Gale makes a note, then looks up to notice that Vic has slunk into his chair after storming out during the discussion on the sales figures. Looking somewhat discomfited, he mumbles, "I guess I should be here — it is my office we're talking about."

"Thanks, Vic. I know it's stressful to be asked to relocate. What are *you* looking for in your office space?"

It doesn't take Vic long to recover from the embarrassment of his earlier outburst. He sits tall in his chair, pauses, and surveys the room for several seconds before replying. "The usual in an office, for the most part. Some privacy to make phone calls and enough space to keep my files. The main thing you folks have to realize is that sales is about image as well as the product. When I bring customers in, they need to see that we're a serious player in the flaxseed oil game — and that they're dealing with someone of substance in the company, not just some order taker."

"You want your office to give your customers a sense of professionalism and to let them know they are important to us as a company."

"Right. Taking them to a cubbyhole at the back just doesn't cut it," Vic responds. "I need the office to be somewhere near the front, big enough to sit comfortably with a couple of clients. And another thing: we have to do something about that warehouse. It's a mess — and dangerous. I feel embarrassed taking customers back there."

Gale anticipates Doug's rebuttal, nods to him reassuringly, and continues with a smile. "Careful, Vic. I think you and Doug actually agree on something — cutting down the traffic in the back."

"Careful, Vic. I think you and Doug actually agree on something."

UNCOVERING INTERESTS

By remaining curious during the discussion about the location of Vic's office, Gale uncovered the following interests:

- Dinah wanted privacy and accessibility to a photocopier and supplies
- Melanie fought for quiet and a sense of personal space
- Doug strove for efficient use of space, organization, and less disruption
- Vic wanted a professional image for customers and accessibility to samples

These interests laid the foundation for the Turm-Oil staff to resolve the issue of Vic's office with the help of a resourceful architect. They moved the warehouse wall opposite Perry's office a couple of feet to widen the hallway area. This allowed them to install shelving and a counter, to which they moved the photocopier and office supplies. They then added some shelving that allowed Doug to get significant product off the warehouse floor and to store other miscellaneous clutter. The samples were moved into a glass case in the boardroom. The former photocopy and supply area next to Dinah's office was converted into an office for Vic.

This collaborative approach resulted in a solution that met the needs of all involved.

- Dinah maintained her office and retained accessibility to the photocopier and supplies, now stored on the new shelving and counter space opposite her office
- Melanie retained her quiet and workspace
- Doug lost some square footage in the warehouse to the widening of the hallway, but the new shelving allowed him to get some pallets off the floor and improved efficiency, while the relocation of the samples to the boardroom greatly reduced warehouse foot traffic
- Vic got an office that presented a professional image and he has the option of meeting customers in the boardroom, with the samples close at hand

Not only did the staff reach a solution that the architect modestly described as "elegant," they also did it in a way in which everyone had a voice. As each person told their story, they felt included and respected. They would be unlikely to harbor the residual hostility and resentment that can linger following a confrontation or grudging compromise. A decision foisted upon people may gain compliance, but a decision in which they are involved will gain their commitment.

BEYOND RIGHT AND WRONG

Positions tether us to the drama triangle. At its simplest, a position says, "I'm right, you're wrong." This moral certainty and righteousness also translate as "I'm the hero, you're the villain."

When we redefine a problem in terms of interests and needs rather than positions, we look beyond right and wrong. We focus on the problem and no longer need to attack the person. While positions result in either/or thinking, interests and needs breed flexibility and cooperation. They allow us to relinquish the roles of hero, victim, and villain and become partners in solving the problem.

FIGURE 11A
FOCUSING ON INTERESTS AND NEEDS

Summary

Conflict often is marked by people dug in on their positions. A position can be defined as a person's desired solution in conflict and does not necessarily consider other people or their needs. A positional attitude reflects a belief that our perspective is "the truth."

We can shift the focus of conflict away from positions by identifying the issue we need to resolve and the topics we need to discuss.

Positions are a means to an end and are motivated by interests and needs. When we frame conflict in terms of each person's interests and needs, we foster better understanding, allow common ground to emerge, and create previously unseen possibilities for resolution.

From theory to practice

Analyze a conflict in which you currently are involved (or that you are witnessing).

- How would you summarize each person's position?
- In neutral and objective terms, what would you list as the issues to be resolved, the topics to be discussed?
- What interests or needs motivated each person to adopt their position?
- What options might meet the needs of both people?

CHAPTER 12

PROBING THE DEPTHS OF CONFLICT

I keep six honest serving men
(They taught me all I knew);
Their names are What and Why and When
And How and Where and Who.
                    — Rudyard Kipling, *The Elephant's Child*

Shifting judgment to curiosity

The roles of the drama triangle blind us to the whole story. Donning the hero's cloak of righteousness, we justify our position and attack that of our adversary. As victim, smarting from being attacked, we focus on defending ourselves. And in the heat of the moment with emotions running high, we may slip into the villain role, intent on punishing our foe. Each of these roles produces judgment that locks us into confrontation.

Judgment leads to a shortsightedness that prevents both understanding and resolution. We focus on symptoms and ignore root causes. Yet, just like an iceberg, most of the conflict lies unseen at first glance. When we fail to grasp or understand the real issues, resolution becomes impossible. We may remain at an impasse, entrenched in our positions. One person may give in or walk away (still feeling resentful). Or we may strike a grudging compromise, though such solutions often are short-lived, as discussed in the previous chapter. Since these outcomes fail to uncover and address the unmet needs that fueled the conflict in the first place, they are unlikely to result in long-term resolution.

If we are able to shift our judgment to curiosity, a couple of things happen. First, we can admit to ourselves, however reluctantly, that the other person has their own story about the conflict. And we can be sure that in their story we have been denied the coveted role of the victim and instead been cast as the villain. No wonder we are reluctant to acknowledge their side of the story! But if we can stifle our self-righteousness long enough to hear their story, we will better understand the impact of the conflict on them and the intent behind their actions. We will be less likely to see (and treat) them as the villain. Walls will become bridges.

Second, we might actually learn something — a radical thought, I know. The other person might provide information that dramatically changes our perspective on the situation. And by remaining curious we can understand their motivation and uncover their interests and needs. New information might reveal previously unseen possibilities for resolution. One way to flex our curiosity muscle is to learn to ask appropriate questions.

All questions are not created equal

In adversarial conflict resolution (epitomized by the courts), people seldom ask questions out of curiosity. Their goal instead is to discredit their adversary's ideas or reinforce their own position. Trial lawyers are told: "Never ask a question unless you already know the answer."

In collaborative conflict resolution, however, our goal is quite different. We seek to increase understanding and to work with the other person against the *problem*. "Winning" is redefined as finding a solution that satisfies the needs of both people. Our questions, therefore, aim to uncover information and bring interests and needs to the surface.

CLOSED QUESTIONS (AND WHY TO AVOID THEM)

Closed (or closed-ended) questions are those that demand a yes or no answer. As their name implies, they attempt to narrow the other person's reply rather than encourage them to tell their story in their own words.

Closed questions normally contain judgments and assumptions that trigger defensiveness. Consider the following question: "Do you think your suggestion is fair to the rest of the staff?" Implicit in the question is the judgment "I don't think your suggestion is fair to the rest of the staff." The person being asked is almost guaranteed to respond defensively and either justify their suggestion or minimize staff concerns.

Other times, people don't even hear a closed question as a question. What would go through your head if your boss asked you: "Can you have this completed by 3:00?" Most of us would interpret this question as "Do this by 3:00!" and respond accordingly. Simply put, if you want to convey information, tell the other person what you need. Your boss would communicate more clearly if he said something like "I need this for a meeting at 3:00. Please make sure it's finished by then." If we want information from another person, we should ask them an open-ended question: "How does 3:00 work for you?" or "What help would you need?" A closed question usually tells you more about the person asking it than about the person answering it.

OPEN-ENDED QUESTIONS (AND WHY THEY WORK)

Just as closed questions tend to limit the responder (and push the agenda of the questioner), open-ended (or open) questions invite the other person to answer in their own words. Such questions are a powerful tool to help us understand another person and their story.

Open-ended questions also are known as "journalistic" questions and begin with one of the following:

Who?	What?	When?
Where?	How?	Why?

One caution about "why" questions: they often create defensiveness and lead the responder to feel it's necessary to justify their position. I believe this reaction stems from childhood experiences. Parents who asked, "Why haven't you cleaned your room?" or "Why did you take the last cookie?" seldom asked out of curiosity. These experiences carry forward into adulthood, and it's easy to see that "whys invite alibis." I'm not suggesting you discard "why" questions, only that you be sure to ask them with genuine curiosity. You may choose to substitute questions such as "What led you to that decision?" or "How did you arrive at that conclusion?"

Peeling the onion for the real story

Open questions allow us to uncover and understand the other person's story. As outlined in Chapter 3, there are three elements to a conflict story: the plot (facts), the characters (emotions/thoughts), and the theme (unmet needs/conflict). The facts are a natural starting point, but until we discover the other person's thoughts and feelings, we cannot really understand the entire story. Ultimately we will need to find out what fueled the conflict — their unmet needs — and what will be required

"Why didn't you tell me earlier that those spreadsheets weren't going to be ready?"

to resolve it. Some people liken this probing to peeling the layers of an onion to get to the heart of the matter (with the occasional tear along the way).

"JUST THE FACTS, MA'AM"

Sergeant Friday of "Dragnet" was famous for refocusing witnesses to stick to what they saw and heard: "Just the facts." Open questions can focus on facts — what was said and done. This focus often clarifies assumptions and ensures both people are looking at the same picture. Some examples:

- "When do you need the report?"
- "What was your understanding of each of our roles on the project?"

- "What led you to feel that I undermined you?"
- "Who else is affected by this procedure?"
- Or, when dealing with someone who is angry, you could ask something as simple as "What happened?" or "What's up?"

WHAT'S GOING ON INSIDE?

Emotions, especially in the workplace, often are minimized or disregarded. Most people are uncomfortable with them and find it far easier to assume they know how someone feels than to ask. As discussed in Chapter 5, our assumptions usually are based on how someone's actions impact us and often are inaccurate. We don't really know how someone is feeling or what motivated their behavior until we ask them. When we take that risk, we often discover that someone's motive was dramatically different from what we assumed. When we hear their side of the story, previously incomprehensible behavior may begin to make sense. Open questions are a powerful tool to bring to the surface underlying feelings and intentions. Questions such as the following encourage the other person to speak directly to their experience and intent:

- "What prompted you to raise the issue in front of the whole team?"
- "What were you intending to convey with your comments?"
- "What motivated you to ask for a transfer?"

Questions that delve into emotions also deepen the conversation. Emotional connections often can build trust and foster understanding. When strong emotions are unaddressed, they will fester and likely block communication and resolution. Questions such as the following can elicit feelings:

- "How do you feel about the new policy?"
- "What went on for you when your report was criticized?"
- "What was it like for you when they hired someone from outside the department to be team leader?"

THE HEART OF CONFLICT — UNMET NEEDS

The theme of a conflict story stems from unmet needs. Conflict would be a lot simpler to resolve if we were aware of our needs and willing to express them directly and respectfully. Unfortunately, this seldom is the case. Most of us react emotionally in conflict. We know we are frustrated but we may be unable to determine or articulate what we need. Rather, we may impulsively vent our frustration by attacking, blaming, or demanding.

Consider, for example, someone who felt shut down or embarrassed at a team meeting. Rarely have I heard someone say: "I'm angry about the way I was treated in that meeting. I need to have my ideas heard and respected." More likely we would hear: "That boss of mine is such a jerk. He dumps all over anyone who disagrees with him."

Open questions are key to uncovering the interests and needs that fuel people's emotions and drive them to adopt strong positions. Examine some of Gale Reasoner's questions in resolving the dispute over where to locate Vic's office:

- "Why next to Melanie, Dinah?"
- "Melanie, you seemed pretty adamant you don't want Vic up front. How come?"
- "Doug ... clearly that's a concern for you. In what way?"
- "Vic, what are *you* looking for in your office space?"

By inviting the other person to articulate their needs directly, these types of questions help reveal the root of the conflict and lay the foundation for resolution.

TIPS ON PROBING

Asking questions is as much an art as a science. Through practice, we can learn to ask questions that gather valuable information. When we add genuine curiosity and trust our instincts (not our impulses), we can achieve the depth of understanding that can transform conflicts. Here are some tips.

"Melanie, you seemed pretty adamant you don't want Vic up front. How come?"

When confronted by a position, ask the person what is important to them and why. Seek to understand what is motivating them to adopt their position.

- "What's important to you about ...?"
- "In what ways would that improve efficiency?"

Conflict often is prolonged when people use a common term but attach different meanings to it. Ask the other person to define a term.

- "What do you mean by [practical]?"
- "What does [teamwork] mean to you?"

We often assume people think the same way we do. Instead of making assumptions, explore their thought process.

- "How did you arrive at that conclusion?"
- "What led you to that conclusion?"
- "When did you arrive at that view?"

Finally, conflict is extremely personal. People adopt positions based on personal experiences. When someone demonstrates passion toward an issue or a position, find out how it affects them personally.

- "How does that affect you?"
- "What are your concerns about ...?"
- "When does that impact you?"
- "How would that benefit you?"
- "What would you be looking to achieve by ...?"

I'll show you mine if ...

Imagine your boss asking you, "Are you happy in your job?" For those of us who value continued employment, the right answer likely would be "Yes, boss." Even the open-ended version — "How are you feeling about your job?" — still would have us wondering, "Why is he asking?" or "What's her agenda?" Depending on our history and relationship with our boss, we might assume the worst and become defensive and guarded.

A question, by its very nature, asks the person being questioned to reveal something. And when we view the person asking the question as our conflict villain, we are understandably reluctant to reveal ourselves. We can reduce this suspicion and mistrust by letting the other person know our reason for asking a question. Before asking an employee how they are doing, a manager might say, "I've noticed you've been very quiet recently. What's up?" Before requesting a rush job, she might say, "I need the report for a meeting with the director at 3:00. How does that fit with your workload today?" Danaan Parry addressed this need for transparency in his book *Warriors of the Heart*:

> The cardinal rule for asking questions is: Give something of yourself before you demand anything of someone else. If you want to know what's going on for another person, then tell them what is going on with you first. Only then do you have the right to ask your question.

Ask only if you really want to know

I mentioned earlier that our words comprise only a small part of the message people receive from us. Our attitude, as reflected in our facial expression and tone of voice, speaks more loudly than our words. I remember an incident years ago in which my attitude was incongruent with my words. After a tense morning with my wife, I remember asking her, "What's *your* problem?" (heavy emphasis on the "your"). Technically this is an open-ended question, though I admit that I was far from curious at the time. Not surprisingly, my wife picked up on this lack of congruence and reacted with a terse defensiveness. (The answer, for the record, was that *I* was the problem, but that story is best left untold.)

When I recounted this incident to a colleague and commented that "these open questions aren't all they're cracked up to be," he took me seriously and suggested I could have asked her, "What's up?" At that point, I had to sheepishly admit that I didn't really want to know "what was up," but wanted to stir the pot, which I managed to do very effectively. This experience reminded me that although conflict resolution skills are important, they will be ineffective unless we apply them with sincerity and curiosity.

Summary

Closed questions normally contain judgments and assumptions that trigger defensiveness. They often reflect the agenda of the person asking the question.

We can get to the core of a conflict by "peeling the layers of the onion" through asking high-yield, open-ended questions. The facts are a natural starting point, but until we discover the other person's thoughts, feelings, and unmet needs, we cannot really understand the entire story.

We reduce suspicion and mistrust by letting the other person know our reason for asking a question.

From theory to practice

Over the next 24 hours, ask only open-ended questions.

Next time you are in conversation (without the pressure of a conflict), ask the other person questions that explore feelings and underlying needs.

Listen for the types of questions asked in media interviews. Assess which ones elicit deeper understanding of the subject and which ones evoke cliché answers.

CHAPTER 13

STANDING UP FOR OURSELVES (WITHOUT KNOCKING THE OTHER PERSON DOWN)

What we don't say controls us.

An alternative to fight or flight

Many people mistakenly believe that collaborative conflict resolution is about being nice — about giving in to make the other person happy and avoid conflict. Far from it. Collaboration is about getting what we need, but not at the expense of the other person. If we ignore our own needs, any solution will be tainted by resentment and frustration. Assertion of our own needs is a key component in any collaborative resolution.

Assertiveness also presents us with a constructive alternative to the fight or flight response associated with our anger. Anger is our body's call to action. Our triggers warn us when our values are being threatened and urge us to protect ourselves and what we hold important. Assertiveness allows us to heed this call without unnecessarily escalating a conflict. It means standing up for yourself — without knocking the other person down. We express our feelings, opinions, and wishes directly and respectfully.

Assertiveness reflects an attitude of mutual respect. A colleague, Ed Jackson, summarized the balance between rights and responsibilities that marks assertive behavior:

> You have the right to say what you think and tell others how you feel. You have an obligation to do that respectfully. You have an obligation to listen to what others have to say and how they feel. You have a right to have those things said to you respectfully.

Finally, assertiveness moves us beyond the drama triangle and focuses on interests and needs and on resolution. By speaking up for ourselves we cast aside the role of the passive, powerless victim. We take responsibility for our needs and for the way we allow others to treat us. When we do so without attacking or judging the other person, they are less likely to feel victimized (and to see us as the villain).

Passive behavior

When we remain passive in conflict, we suppress our opinions and needs and feel like the victim. Our gremlins caution us, "This isn't safe" or "What if they don't like us?" or "Why bother?" Whether to keep the peace or to save ourselves from harm, we allow others to encroach on our rights unchallenged. Even if we choose to say something, it usually is delivered so tentatively or apologetically that others can hardly be expected to take us seriously. After all, if *we* fail to make our needs important, why should someone else? Our self-esteem suffers and our suppressed emotions may lead to resentment and even revenge (passive-aggressive behavior).

Passive behavior also can undermine trust. Think of someone you know whom you would characterize as passive. How much can you rely on them to give you the straight goods when you ask them how things are going for them? They likely will assure you that "everything is fine." And things might be fine, but their tendency to avoid conflict will prevent you from taking their answer at face value.

Aggressive behavior

Just as passive behavior locks us into the role of victim, aggressive behavior locks us into the revolving door of hero and villain. Our gremlins fan our self-righteousness and call for vengeance with phrases such as "We don't have to take that," "I would never do anything like that," and "What a jerk." When we're feeling this way, our ends justify our means and we seek to meet our needs at the expense of the other person. We look to control the other person through put-downs, threats, or intimidation. We are so fixated on winning the argument that we blind ourselves to our own interests and needs.

When we're being aggressive, we deliver our message in a way that leaves no doubt that we see the other person as the villain. They are predictably reluctant to accept this role and feel compelled to defend themselves and their good name. Our message falls on deaf ears. Aggressive behavior also undermines trust, as people are unlikely to trust us if we attack and judge them.

"I" statements

To borrow from Woody Allen, 80 percent of assertiveness is speaking up. Instead of clamming up when faced with conflict, we need to say something, however inarticulate or clumsy our words might seem. We can begin to shed the role of victim with a blunt "I don't like what's happening here" or "I'm getting frustrated with these interruptions." Once we risk speaking up, our challenge is to deliver the message directly yet respectfully. "I" statements help us achieve this balance. Even a statement (such as "That stung!") that does not start with "I" can let the other person know what is going on for us.

"You" statements label and blame the other person. Or they claim to know what the other person thinks or feels ("You obviously don't care about the team"). As detailed in Chapter 10, people react defensively to such accusations. A case in point is Vic's tirade during the quarterly meeting. Vic had several valid points and a key perspective on the issue of lagging sales. Yet the manner in which he made his points antagonized the very people from whom he needed support. His legitimate concerns were ignored in the ensuing defensive scramble. The group failed to define the problem, much less discuss or resolve it. Here are some examples of the "you" statements Vic fired at his colleagues:

"You bean counters are making us look second-rate."

"You guys in the warehouse screw up every second order."

"You people can't even get me brochures for the annual trade show."

"You bean counters are making us look second-rate."

It's not hard to understand why Vic had trouble getting his co-workers to hear him out. Had he, in offering his perspective, changed his blaming "you" statements to "I" statements, he could have told his story in a way the others could hear. They would not have felt the need to defend themselves from his judgments and blame. He could have fully expressed what he saw as the facts, how he felt, and what he needed. Here's how the meeting might have unfolded.

"Look, sales are down — no question. And I'm not happy about it either. I think there are some areas we could work on as a group that would definitely help me in the field and boost sales for the company. One area is our presence in the marketplace. Several customers mentioned they were surprised we weren't represented at the Wellness Show last month, especially when one of the keynote speeches highlighted flaxseed oil. I felt embarrassed but didn't want us to look cheap, so I took the hit and told them I didn't book in time. I'd like to look at some ways we can increase our presence in the marketplace. It would make it a lot easier when I have to call on customers."

"Don't blame me," Perry blurts defensively as his face twitches. "You're not the only one in this office with budget demands. I'm not Santa Claus, you know."

"Perry, I know things are tight. In hindsight, I could have done a better job of letting you know how important this was. I'd like to talk more with you about how we can prioritize these events and get the biggest bang for our buck."

"I'm not Santa Claus, you know."

In this scenario, Vic outlined his concerns, told the group the reasons for those concerns, shared his embarrassment, and asserted his need for higher visibility in the marketplace. Because he didn't blame or judge others, his colleagues were much more receptive to his message.

As always, being genuine is more important than being technically correct. I remember one student who was practicing assertiveness in a situation that was very close to home for her. She was struggling to stay objective and finally glared at her role-play partner and fired back, "You're being a jerk about this." I asked her how she might make her point using an "I" statement instead. She paused a moment. Then her face lit up in what I assumed was an "aha" moment. She turned to her antagonist and confidently said, "*I think* you're being a jerk about this."

The difficult person story
SPREADSHEET SUBTERFUGE: DINAH'S STORY

The clatter of plastic on glass snaps Gale from the daydream induced by the latest workers' compensation board epistle about air quality in the workplace. She turns from the mountain of paper on the boardroom table to catch Dinah fumbling at the display case with several large bottles of SuperFlax oil.

"Hey, Dinah, what's up — besides your blood pressure?" Gale smiles at her own joke. Dinah frowns, however, less than impressed with Gale's attempt to lighten the mood.

"What's up is that you can't turn around in this place without someone putting a knife in your back," she snarls.

Gale's smile quickly fades. "Butting heads with Clyde again? I heard you two getting into it this morning — from across the office."

"Clyde's Clyde." Dinah sighs with a dismissive wave of her hand. "It's little Melanie I'm talking about."

"Melanie? I'm surprised to hear that. She's not one to rock the boat."

Dinah nods emphatically as she warms up to her conflict du jour. "That's exactly my point. She's all Miss Sweetness and Light in public, then pulls the rug out when you're not looking. She's so manipulative. In fact," Dinah's voice drops to a conspiratorial whisper as she leans toward Gale, "I think she's passive-aggressive." Dinah nods knowingly as she delivers her diagnosis.

"I think she's passive-aggressive."

"Something must have happened between you two," Gale responds.

"This morning I gave her some spreadsheets to update for my weekly meeting with Clyde. Not only did she not do them, I was the last to know my work wasn't going to be done. To make matters worse, Clyde used that as a reason to jump all over me. When I defended myself and told him about Melanie, he said, 'That's no excuse. She has other priorities.' You know, she had Doug, of all people, tell Clyde why she didn't do my spreadsheets. I'm the only one around this zoo not to know that *my* work wasn't being done." Dinah's jaw tightens and her face begins to redden.

"It's certainly maddening to be out of the loop, then get blind-sided by Clyde," Gale offers.

"And then to see Melanie skate through this as Miss Innocence. She must have majored in manipulation in that community-college course of hers."

Gale pauses to digest this latest drama. "Let me make sure I understand this. It wasn't as much that she didn't do the work, but that she didn't talk to you directly about it."

"Exactly. I could have done it myself in a pinch — if I'd known. She must have been trying to set me up. She's devious, that one."

"And you'd prefer that Melanie give you a heads-up if there might be problems getting your work done."

"Is that too much to ask?" Dinah implores, as she raises her hands to the heavens and bustles from the room.

SPREADSHEET SUBTERFUGE: MELANIE'S STORY

A few minutes later, Gale's musings are interrupted by a persistent tinkle outside the boardroom door. She glances up to see Melanie absent-mindedly stirring her tea. Gale quietly interrupts. "Careful, Melanie, you'll wear out your favorite cup."

Melanie's head snaps toward Gale and her face flushes as she realizes the extent of her preoccupation. "Oh, sorry, Gale. I was drifting. I just can't get Dinah out of my mind." She draws a deep breath and her normally cheerful face hardens. "She is *such* a difficult person. I mean, I get along with everyone here but she's impossible. Just so demanding and … rude," she stammers. Her shoulders sag and she seems to deflate. "It's just hard to deal with," she sighs.

"Wow. I don't remember seeing you this upset before. What did she do that you see as demanding and rude?"

"It's mainly when she has work for me. Instead of talking to me about it or asking me about priorities, she just drops it on my desk with a note telling me what the deadline is. Like she's the only one I do things for. And then, when I couldn't get it done, she comes out of her meeting with Clyde, gives me a dirty look, and ignores me for the rest of the day."

"She is such a difficult person."

Gale nods. "That would be upsetting. What is it about leaving the note that causes you problems?"

"It makes me feel like I'm her servant. People say we're supposed to be a team, but the way Dinah carries on, they must be talking about some other office. Plus I have projects for Doug and Clyde on the go and they each told me their project was top priority. You know how they are. I didn't know what to do," Melanie sputters, reliving her panic.

"So what did you do?"

"Well, I went to Doug because his project also was due today. I explained that I was in a bind and couldn't do everything. He was really nice and understanding. He told me that Dinah could do her own spreadsheets, that I should stick with his project, and that he would handle things with Clyde and Dinah. I was going to talk to Dinah, but thought I might be able to get her work done for her meeting. Besides, you know how mad she gets when she doesn't get her own way."

Gale draws a breath and reflects for a moment. "So you felt stretched in three different directions and a little intimidated by the prospect of not giving Dinah what she wanted."

Melanie's voice quivers and her eyes moisten ever so slightly. "No matter what I did, someone was going to be mad at me. What could I do?"

"Seems like your main problem with Dinah is that she just drops work on your desk with a deadline, and you'd like to have a chance to discuss and plan priorities with her."

Melanie nods, a bit sheepishly, as if her request were unreasonable. Gale continues, "And you didn't talk to Dinah about it because Doug said he'd handle it — and because you were worried that she might get upset."

"Yes. I didn't want to cause tension between us."

"Seems like you've gotten tension and then some by *not* talking to her. There might not be that much to lose by discussing it with her."

Melanie raises her eyebrows as she reluctantly considers this option. "Maybe. I'll think about it. Anyway, thanks for listening. Oh, and don't tell Dinah about this." Melanie forces a smile and returns to her desk.

"I'm okay. *They* need professional help"

Assertiveness may involve expressing our interests and needs about a specific issue: Vic talking about increasing exposure in the market-place, for example, or Dinah explaining to Gale that her supplies had to be accessible. More frequently, assertiveness addresses how others treat us. (Remember the "process" leg of the wobbly stool?) We sel-dom find others disrespectful or "difficult" simply because they dis-agree with us. Rather, they trigger us because of how they treat us. Think of a person you find difficult. (If they are in the room when you are reading this, act normally and *don't point.*) What two words do you associate with that person?

In doing this exercise with thousands of workshop participants, I've found that the following words continually arise:

controlling	arrogant
stubborn	inconsiderate
manipulative	unreasonable
uncooperative	demanding

These people clearly are villains! Anyone (except them) can see that they deserve our scorn and anything else we can dish out in response to their dysfunctional behavior. As satisfying as this rush of self-righteousness may be, it places us in a no-win situation. If we "tell it like it is," they likely will get defensive and deny our charges, and things probably will get worse. If we don't "tell it like it is," the unacceptable behavior continues. Either way, we remain trapped on the drama triangle, as the victim of their villainy.

But to heed the words of Albert Einstein, we cannot solve prob-lems with the same consciousness that created them. Our view of the "difficult" person will guide our efforts to solve the problem. Some views doom us to spin our wheels and serve only to deepen our frus-tration; other views open new possibilities and allow us to create new outcomes.

Most commonly, we see the *person* as the problem: they are a jerk, an idiot. If the person is the problem, to solve the problem we must either eliminate or avoid them. Elimination (as delicious as it might seem in our darkest fantasies) produces unpleasant legal consequences and leaves us with the further problem of where to hide the body. As for avoidance, if we could avoid such a difficult person, we likely would have done so long ago. Often we find people difficult specifically because we don't have the option of avoiding them.

Alternatively, we may attribute the conflict to the *personality* deficiencies of the other person. They are arrogant, condescending, rude, or inconsiderate. If we view their personality as the problem, we are left with the task of changing their personality. Psychotherapy, electric shock, or a lobotomy might work but normally require the consent of the patient, and no matter how convinced you are that they need professional help, they probably disagree. This view also pegs them as the villain and reinforces our role as the innocent victim.

In our example, both Dinah and Melanie saw each other as the problem. Dinah described Melanie as manipulative, devious, and passive-aggressive. Melanie saw Dinah as demanding and rude. They were destined to remain deadlocked as long as they attributed the conflict to the personality deficiencies of the other person.

Describing the difficult behavior

A third, more productive, approach separates the person from their behavior and focuses on influencing the behavior we find difficult. Although we cannot control another's behavior, we have far more power to influence it than we usually give ourselves credit for.

When we characterize someone as a jerk or a grump, they inevitably balk at being labeled. Even the most unpleasant person does not act that way 24/7. Most people will admit to having a bad day or speaking out of turn, but not to being a bad person. Instead of labeling the person as the villain, we can identify the behavior in question, tell them how it impacts us, and ask them for what we need. Often, they were unaware of what they were doing or its impact on us. They may be shocked or even embarrassed by this realization. If we raise the issue in a way that allows them to save face (i.e., not be cast as the villain), they often will change how they act toward us. Even if the situation is more complicated and they get defensive, we have at least brought the issue to the surface, allowing discussion and, hopefully, resolution. Sometimes the other person may even deny the validity of our concerns in the moment but change how they treat us in the future.

While there are no guarantees that someone else will respond positively to our request, consider the alternative. What message do we send to someone when we *don't* say anything about irritating or inappropriate behavior? Outwardly, our silence implies acceptance. Inwardly, we fume in frustration and judge them. Such judgment seems unfair when we haven't made them aware of our concerns and given them a chance to present their perspective or even to change their behavior once they know it irritates us. Our silence dooms us to remain the victim — innocent, powerless, and continually frustrated.

Instead of judgment or silence, we can use examples to focus the conversation on specific behavior and its impact on us. When we find ourselves frustrated with another person, we can ask ourselves, "What am I seeing and hearing right now that's triggering me?" In the conflict over the spreadsheet, either Dinah or Melanie could have raised the issue assertively by describing the problem behavior. Instead of labeling Melanie as "manipulative," Dinah could have described Melanie's actions ("when you talked to Doug instead of me about work I asked you to do") and requested that Melanie speak to her directly when she had scheduling problems. Similarly, instead of labeling Dinah as "rude," Melanie could have referred to Dinah's dropping work on her desk and asked Dinah to talk to her about assignments when she delivered them. When we frame the problem in terms of behavior, we reduce the defensiveness that inevitably results when people label and judge each other.

Even though being able to describe the problem behavior would have been a significant step for both Dinah and Melanie, they still would have had to tame their conflict gremlins (discussed in Chapter 8) and risk approaching the other person directly about their concerns.

First within, then without

Although we cannot change another person, we can change our reaction to them. Our "difficult" people are those whose behavior triggers us. As discussed in Chapter 7, our sensitivities reflect our previous experiences — the behaviors "trigger" feelings already within us. Since our life experiences vary, so do our triggers; what sets off one person may be admired or appreciated by another. We judge our villain as controlling; others admire them for taking charge. We label someone as arrogant; others see them as confident. The behavior is the same; only our judgment of it differs.

One of the most popular courses I offer is called "Dealing with Difficult People." Many who attend seek a "silver bullet" — an immediate, painless way to change the people they find difficult. Once the workshop starts (and the doors are locked, the registration fees collected) I reveal the workshop's real title: "There Are No Difficult People, Only People I Have Difficulty With." I explain that we can be responsible only for our own feelings and actions, then jokingly ask if anyone wants a refund. So far there have been no tak-ers — only a few sighs of resignation as people realize there is no easy answer. When we find someone difficult, our reaction says more about us than it does about them.

When we identify the behavior we have difficulty with, we can plan a response. Instead of blindly reacting, we can choose thoughts, words, and actions to influence positive change. Even when the other person's behavior persists, we still have choices. We may accept the status quo but decide to view the situation differently. We may be able to look beyond the irritating behavior and discover positive qualities in the other person. We may even see our difficult person as a teacher and reflect on the lesson they are unconsciously offering us. To understand and accept ourselves and others is a lifetime's work. Conflict provides an opportunity to do that work.

The D-E-S statement

One way to formulate our thoughts and present our perspective assertively is through a D-E-S statement (Describe, Express,

Specify). The elements of this action-oriented statement communicate our story honestly and accurately without painting ourselves as the victim or the other person as the villain. This approach moves us beyond the drama triangle by focusing on objective behaviors, interests, and needs.

The D stands for *describe* — to objectively and factually state the words and actions we want to address. By reporting what we heard or saw, we minimize the judgment and generalizations that trigger defensiveness in our listener. Vic demonstrated this in the "after" version of the discussion about the sales figures when he replaced "You bean counters are making us look second-rate" with a more objective "Several customers mentioned they were surprised we weren't represented at the Wellness Show last month." Vic simply presented information instead of casting blame. His story had no villains. Even though Perry reacted defensively at first, Vic had laid an objective foundation of customer feedback that eliminated unnecessary argument over the value of the Wellness Show and allowed the discussion to focus on Perry's concerns about the budget.

The E in the D-E-S statement refers to the need to *express* the impact the behavior has had on us. In some cases it might be appropriate to let the other person know how we felt (Vic's "I felt embarrassed"). Other times, we might not feel safe or be inclined to share our feelings, in which case we can express our reaction to their behavior ("I shut down when I get yelled at" or "I have a hard time staying focused with these personal attacks"). Such statements help clarify assumptions (Chapter 5) by letting the other person know how their behavior impacts us. When we take responsibility for our feelings and reactions without blaming the other person, we move ourselves out of the role of victim and often begin to build empathy.

Finally, the S reminds us to *specify* what we need or prefer (Vic's "I'd like to look at some ways we can increase our presence in the marketplace"). Specifying a need or preference shouldn't be used as a fancy way to hammer home a position or judgment. "I need you not to be a jerk" remains aggressive. "I need the corner office" doesn't leave as much room for options as does "I need ample space to meet with my team." However, when we ask directly for what we need, we shed the role of victim and empower ourselves.

Let's return to the example of the conflict between Dinah and Melanie. Each experienced the other as a difficult person and each felt frustrated with the other. Either one of them could have initiated a respectful and productive conversation about their communication problem. Melanie might have started with: "Dinah, I'd like to discuss how work is delivered to me. Rather than getting a note, I'd like the chance to talk with you when you give me assignments, especially when things are busy. I want to do a good job for everyone and I have to juggle priorities."

"I'd like the chance to talk with you when you give me assignments."

Dinah also could have approached Melanie. She could have said, "Look, Melanie, I want to clear the air from yesterday. I was really ticked off that I was the last to know my work wasn't going to be done. If you have problems, please come to me directly so we can try to sort them out. At least I'll know what's up when I report to Clyde." Someone needed to take the initiative and be assertive.

When the other person doesn't respond

Even when we directly and respectfully ask for what we need, there is no guarantee we will get it. Others may be unwilling or even unable to change. Our efforts, however, can bear fruit in other ways. First, by raising an issue assertively with the other person we discover where we stand with them. We can then choose alternatives to collaboration: we can ask for the help of a third party, transfer to another department, lodge a formal complaint, or terminate a relationship. In considering options, ask yourself, "How can I best get my needs met *without* the cooperation of the other person?"

Second, assertiveness goes hand in glove with self-esteem. When we speak up for our needs, we are being true to ourselves. When I haven't spoken up, I usually replay an unpleasant encounter over and over in my mind (with the color commentary of my gremlins). When I have expressed what was true for me at the time, I can more easily let go of the encounter.

In some conversations, the other person may persist with unacceptable behavior even after we have acknowledged their concerns and set limits. In such cases we have every right to terminate the conversation. However, where an ongoing relationship is involved, such as with a customer, client, or co-worker, we can do this in a way that invites future conversation. To simply hang up or terminate a meeting would further trigger the other person's sense of powerlessness and disconnection, reinforcing their role as victim. Such an abrupt response makes it awkward for either person to rekindle communication. But by saying something like "I told you I'm not willing to be sworn at. Call me back this afternoon. Good-bye," we leave the door open to talk again. The subsequent conversation will inevitably be more productive and may even include an apology from the other person once they have descended anger mountain and reflected on their behavior.

A few tips

Be prepared to repeat yourself. Be persistent.

Treat the D-E-S statement as a smorgasbord. You may need to use only part of it ("I need to finish what I'm saying"). Or you may find it more natural to change the order ("I need to slow things down here. I get overwhelmed when three people talk at once").

Balance assertiveness with empathy. Leave space in the conversation for the other person to respond.

Summary

Assertiveness means expressing our feelings, opinions, and wishes directly and respectfully. It allows us to tell our story in a way that doesn't cast the other person as the villain.

"You" statements label and blame the other person, fostering defensiveness. "I" statements focus on our own experience.

Instead of attributing a problem to the personality flaws of the other person and labeling them as the villain, focus on their behavior — their words and actions.

One way to formulate our thoughts and present our perspective assertively is through a D-E-S statement (Describe, Express, Specify). Tell the other person what you see and hear, how you feel, and what you need.

Balance assertiveness with empathy to allow the other person to tell their story as well.

From theory to practice

Consider a "difficult" person in your life.

- What behaviors make the person difficult for you (be specific and objective)?
- What do you think motivates them to act the way they do (keep in mind that all behavior makes sense)?
- What is the impact of those behaviors on you? How do you react or feel?
- How do you think the other person perceives you? What could you do to alter or correct that perception?
- What do you need from that person to improve communication and work more effectively with them to problem solve?
- What might stop you from asking them directly for what you need?
- What would be the cost of *not* asking them directly for what you need?

CHAPTER 14

THE ROAD TO RESOLUTION

Nature does not hurry, yet everything is accomplished.
— Lao Tzu

When undertaking any journey, especially one fraught with the challenges and pitfalls that conflict presents, it's always good to have a plan and even better to have a map. One of my colleagues, mediator and trainer Brian Frank, likens the conflict resolution process to driving a car. He notes the value of having an overall plan, while cautioning us to keep our eyes on the road and respond to what we notice. In the same spirit, I suggest you use the process outlined in this chapter as a guide, but focus on being mindful in the moment and trusting your instincts.

Having an overall plan when we enter conflict resolution provides a sense of direction and can help us avoid a common pitfall. Most students I've taught share a counterproductive tendency. They leap to solutions and figure out what *should* be done before fully understanding either the problem or the other person's perspective. Some problems are easily solved, but most conflicts are more complicated. When we focus on symptoms and ignore root causes, we shouldn't be surprised when the conflict resurfaces in some other way. The tendency to get ahead of ourselves also works against us when the other person jumps to a different solution. We get locked into positions before exploring the interests on which solutions should be based. As Stephen Covey counsels in his *Seven Habits of Highly Effective People,* "Diagnose before you prescribe." A road map can remind us to do just that.

Earlier, we observed the staff at Turm-Oil Inc. when they were asked to find office space for Vic. Each jumped in with their own solution. Dinah immediately suggested that Vic move next to Melanie, who reacted with her own solution that Dinah should just move the photocopier and supplies. And on it went. Discussion quickly degenerated into argument and ultimately a deadlock broken only by Clyde's decree that Vic would use the boardroom. In the second meeting, Gale set a different context for the discussion and led the group through a collaborative conflict resolution process. She focused on the issue at hand and provided everyone with an opportunity to share their perspective and state their needs. Once this was done, the group explored new possibilities and ultimately arrived at a creative solution endorsed by everyone.

As we examine the steps in the conflict resolution process we'll see how Doug Right was able to apply them to deal more effectively with Marko Blunt and Big Bob's Banana Blend order.

Preparing to meet

Before we leave on a trip, we pack our bags. Ironically, the road to resolution requires us to *unpack* our bags before we leave.

Though some conflicts occur spontaneously and may catch us by surprise, most issues simmer long enough to allow us to plan how to approach them. Unpacking our personal "baggage" allows us to move beyond the roles of the drama triangle before we engage the other person. If we don't shed those roles, we will approach the conflict as a victim and, by extension, see and treat the other person as a villain. Preparation encourages us to replace judgment with curiosity and empathy. When we move beyond the drama triangle, we encourage the other person to move with us in collaboration.

Through some mental preparation, we also can anticipate where and when we might feel triggered and how we tend to react in those situations. We can then strategize how best to manage ourselves and respond constructively when dealing with those sensitive areas. As discussed in Chapter 8, we'll have conversations with our gremlins. Better to have them in private than during a discussion with another person.

Here are some questions to ask yourself before you meet with someone to resolve a conflict:

- What's my purpose in meeting/speaking with the other person?
- Why do I want to approach this collaboratively? What's in it for them to work this out?
- When and where should we meet?
- What might I say to them to set a positive tone?
- In general terms, what is this about?
- Specifically, what aspects of the situation do we need to talk about?
- When did the knife go in from my perspective? What interests and needs lie at the heart of the issue for me? What's important to me?
- When might the knife have gone in for them? What might have triggered them? What might be important to them?
- What interests and needs might we have in common?
- What might they not understand about my perspective?

Doug's preparation to meet with Marko

Here's what Doug might have come up with (with Gale's help) in preparing to meet with Marko over the incomplete order and the complaint from Big Bob's Health Emporium.

What's my purpose in meeting/speaking with Marko?

To find out what happened, resolve the problem with Big Bob, and make sure the same thing doesn't happen again.

Why do I want to approach this collaboratively? What's in it for Marko to work this out?

For me, Marko will be a big part of any solution, especially to make sure this doesn't happen again. For Marko, I know he doesn't like getting yelled at by Big Bob.

When and where should we meet?

Probably best to wait until after the courier has gone for the day so Marko won't be stressed or preoccupied. We should meet somewhere other than my office. Maybe we could take a walk or grab a coffee across the street so we won't be interrupted.

What might I say to Marko to set a positive tone?

I could let him know that this isn't about pointing fingers, but about improving things in the future. I also could acknowledge that Big Bob is a tough guy to deal with.

In general terms, what is this about?

Big Bob's order.

Specifically, what aspects of the situation do we need to talk about?

We need to talk about what happened with the order and the missing product, about what Marko said to Big Bob, and about the system we have in place for orders.

When did the knife go in from my perspective? What interests and needs lie at the heart of the issue for me? What's important to me?

The knife went in for me when Big Bob phoned and tore a strip off me. I need to be able to rely on Marko and to have confidence in our system when a customer complains. As a company, we need satisfied customers. The knife went in again when Marko delayed shipping the rest of the order because I was in a meeting.

"I wonder what's going on for Marko."

When might the knife have gone in for Marko? What might have triggered him? What might be important to him?

Probably when Big Bob accused him of shorting the order. Knowing Marko, he probably got triggered when Big Bob wouldn't listen to his side of the story.

What interests and needs might we have in common?

We're both proud of the jobs we do and want to look good to others in the company and to our customers. We also don't want to have to listen to Big Bob bad-mouth us.

What might Marko not understand about my perspective?

Marko might not realize that I need to have details of the orders and confidence in the system before I can go to bat for him. I wanted to support him but didn't think I had a leg to stand on.

By spending time considering these aspects of the situation, Doug broadened his perspective, clarified his own needs, and began to open to Marko's side of the story. Instead of barging forward, he developed a strategy to approach and resolve the problem cooperatively.

Steps to collaboration

Here are five recommended steps on the road to resolution. Each step has a purpose and will help you to identify, understand, and resolve a conflict. If you skip or gloss over a step, you may find yourself rubbing elbows again with those pesky victims, villains, and heroes and experiencing the confrontation they create.

1. SETTING THE STAGE (HOW ARE WE GOING TO APPROACH THIS?)

When we set the stage, we build a foundation for discussion, exploration of the issue, and, ultimately, resolution. The opening few minutes of a conversation are crucial to establishing a positive, collaborative tone that creates a "safe space" for the conflict to exist — one in which each person can share their perspective and voice their concerns.

To help establish this positive climate, we can let the other person know why we are raising an issue (to clear the air, improve the working relationship, build understanding). This step is particularly important where tension exists as a result of our history with the other person. There is a saying, "When there is an elephant in the room, give it a name." You've likely been in situations where everyone present felt a tension between two people but everyone pretended nothing was wrong. The more such tension is ignored, the more it grows until it is like an elephant in the room, taking up space and causing us to tiptoe around it. The simple act of "naming the elephant" allows it to be discussed and reduces the space and energy it consumes. By clarifying our intention, we can reduce the defensiveness that flows from the other person's assumption that we are a villain who has come to attack or judge them.

We also can reset the stage and revisit this step whenever we need to defuse emotion or re-establish a collaborative tone. If we fail to create a collaborative atmosphere, suspicion and defensiveness will hamper any subsequent conversation.

This step also ensures we agree with the other person on the confidentiality of the discussion, the length of the meeting, whether we'll take notes, and the possibility of follow-up meetings if we're unable to resolve the matter in one meeting.

In Chapter 6, we watched Doug approach Marko the day after their initial confrontation. He invited Marko to go for a walk — a neutral, private location that had them talking more as equals and de-emphasized the supervisor/employee dynamic that meeting in Doug's office reinforced. (Doug was careful not to frame this as an invitation to "step outside and settle this.") He asked whether Marko had 15 minutes. He also reassured Marko that this was not about discipline but about sorting out the problem.

Most important, Doug "named the elephant" and took responsibility for his role in the previous day's blow-up. He acknowledged he had been angry and failed to listen to Marko. He expressed his sincere desire to revisit the situation and work with Marko to make sure the problem didn't happen again. In doing so, he set the stage for a productive discussion and encouraged Marko to tell his story.

"First, I want to apol ..."

2. SHARING OUR STORIES (HOW DO WE EACH SEE THE SITUATION?)

In conflict, everyone has their own story. People need an opportunity to tell their story and need to know it has been heard. We enhance the collaborative climate when each person has a chance to present their perspective without being judged or corrected. Listening does not mean agreement. Our goal is understanding.

In our example, Marko remained somewhat suspicious despite Doug's attempts to foster a collaborative climate. To build trust, Doug had to prove he wanted the conversation to be different by first just listening.

"I know. Tell you what — I'll shut up, you tell me what happened with Big Bob, then I'll tell you my side. How does that sound?" After Doug heard Marko out, he clarified a few details and then summarized to make sure he fully understood Marko's experience. By then, Marko felt heard and was willing to listen to Doug's concerns. This step gave each of them a broader perspective on the problem facing them.

3. CREATING AN AGENDA (WHAT DO WE NEED TO DISCUSS AND RESOLVE?)

Most people have suffered through meetings without an agenda. The resulting lack of focus wastes tremendous time and energy as the group jumps from one issue to another without resolving any of them. I've heard of people scheduling root canal surgery to avoid such meetings.

Once you've heard each other's story, take a minute to ensure you and the other person fully agree on what you need to discuss and resolve. Sometimes this is straightforward — you may be meeting over a single issue that is clear to each of you ("I'd like to talk about what happened between us at the staff meeting yesterday"). In other cases, there may be several aspects to the problem ("I'd like to define our roles in the warehouse and discuss use of the forklift"). Also, the other person may have issues of which you aren't yet aware ("While we're at it, I have concerns about overtime"). Even a simple agenda can help to focus the conversation and still leave room for new issues that neither person may have anticipated ("I guess we need to figure out how this will affect the budget").

By emphasizing neutral topics, the agenda shifts the focus from the positions on the drama triangle to understanding the problem that needs to be resolved. Chapter 11 discussed the value of framing a conflict in terms of neutral topics that provide everyone with an opportunity to express their opinions. Keep agenda issues short and simple so they may serve as a framework for the deeper discussion to follow.

You may find it helpful to write down the topics on a whiteboard, flip chart, notepad, or even a restaurant napkin, depending on the circumstances. Having a written agenda reassures each person that topics important to them won't be forgotten. It also encourages people to focus on their mutual problem rather than to attack each other — a powerful demonstration of "separating the person from the problem."

After Doug set a collaborative tone when he approached Marko the second time, he invited Marko to talk about "what happened with Big Bob" the previous day. As Marko provided more information, Doug identified two issues: how to ensure orders were complete before they were shipped and how to document what was included in each order. Identifying the issues reassured Marko that Doug was listening, focused them both on the problem, and broke the problem into manageable chunks.

4. EXPLORING INTERESTS AND NEEDS (WHAT DO WE EACH NEED IN A SOLUTION?)

This exploration shifts us off the drama triangle into the circle of resolution. It provides each of us with an opportunity to deepen our understanding of the situation, including when the knife went in, how the situation affected us, and what we need to move forward.

Here we uncover the interests and needs underlying the positions that lock us into confrontation. The open-ended questions discussed in Chapter 12 and active curiosity help us as we peel the layers of the onion to find out what is important to the other person and why. At the same time, we need to balance curiosity with a willingness to disclose our own interests, needs, feelings, and perspectives. By both listening and talking, we bring to the surface our full stories, particularly the unmet needs that fueled the conflict.

People frequently shortchange this exploration in their haste to problem solve, but attempts to quick-fix the problem often result in retrenching of positions. A rush toward solution focuses exclusively on the content of the conflict and ignores process and emotions — two-thirds of the three-legged stool presented in Chapter 6. When these legs are ignored, we may find the other person resistant to even a well-intentioned suggestion because they feel unheard or angry.

Doug and Marko's talk and walk in the "back forty" provided each of them with a more complete version of the Big Bob's Banana Blend story. They were able to fill in missing pieces of information and clarify assumptions. They clarified what each of them needed in a solution: they both wanted to ensure orders were complete when they went out; Marko needed a solution that was efficient ("Then I got to move the stuff twice. Takes too long"), as did Doug ("But now that I think about it, it's crazy to have me sign off everything when I'm in so many meetings"). Doug also needed some way to verify orders so he could respond to customer complaints.

"Then I got to move the stuff twice."

5. SOLVING THE PROBLEM (WHAT ARE OUR OPTIONS AND WHO WILL DO WHAT BY WHEN?)

We're ready to problem solve only when we can summarize the problem in terms of interests and needs. Completing this step ensures that we have moved beyond the drama triangle of right and wrong and redefined "winning" as getting what we need.

Sometimes our exploration in the previous step sheds a new light on the problem so that a solution becomes obvious. Other times, brainstorming will create options to which our positions have previously blinded us. We can evaluate these options against the interests and needs uncovered during the exploration phase. ("I don't see how your suggestion will allow us to verify the orders" or "From my perspective, that wouldn't give us the efficiency we're looking for.") The synergy of collaboration often involves taking parts of several ideas and creating a more complete and imaginative solution.

To complete the problem-solving process, we need to make any agreement or understanding explicit. Clarify "who will do what by when." Without a concrete outcome, we may have just had a "nice" conversation without producing a meaningful change. Clarification also prevents things from slipping between the cracks. Sometimes our next step may be to gather information and meet again. Each time we make and honor a commitment to one another, we build trust.

When Doug wrapped up his meeting with Marko, he clarified that "I'll check with Lance and Melanie to make sure this works for them, then e-mail everyone to keep them in the loop. You talk to the courier guys and tell them we're trying out the color-coding."

The conflict resolution two-step

Each step in the process of resolving a conflict builds on the previous step and serves to focus our energy. The natural flow of conversation, however, is unlikely to be sequential and we need to remain flexible and responsive. Some people liken conflict resolution to a dance — there are established steps, but it is much more important to "dance with who brung you" and respond to your partner in the moment. In this spirit, we do not need to view the process as strictly linear and can always revisit a step as the situation requires.

Anytime we need to clarify the process or re-establish a cooperative tone, for example, we can return to setting the stage. Similarly, our agenda should be a work in progress, to be expanded if new topics arise in the course of our discussions. We may even be discussing options to solve the problem only to find that we need to explore the problem further ("What do you mean by efficiency?"). The process simply provides a focus for whatever needs to be done in the moment and an overall plan for our discussion.

Summary

The road map to conflict resolution includes the following steps:

1. Setting the stage (How are we going to approach this?)
2. Sharing our stories (How do we each see the situation?)
3. Creating an agenda (What do we need to discuss and resolve?)
4. Exploring interests and needs (What do we each need in a solution?)
5. Solving the problem (What are our options and who will do what by when?)

It's okay to retrace your steps (but try to avoid stepping on toes as you do).

From theory to practice

Next time you intend to approach someone to raise an issue or resolve a conflict, use the following guide to prepare yourself:

- What's my purpose in meeting/speaking with the other person?
- Why do I want to approach this collaboratively? What's in it for them to work this out?
- When and where should we meet?
- What might I say to them to set a positive tone?
- In general terms, what is this about?
- Specifically, what aspects of the situation do we need to talk about?
- When did the knife go in from my perspective? What interests and needs lie at the heart of the issue for me? What's important to me?
- When might the knife have gone in for them? What might have triggered them? What might be important to them?
- What interests and needs might we have in common?
- What might they not understand about my perspective?

Using a past conflict as an example, reflect on the road map. In what ways did you apply the principles outlined in each step? What steps did you skip or shortchange? How did that impact the discussion? Looking at the steps can be especially helpful to understanding where a conversation may have gone awry.

CHAPTER 15

TIPS FOR THE TRAVELER

It's a dangerous business, Frodo, going out your door.
You step onto the Road, and if you don't keep your feet,
there's no knowing where you might be swept off to.
— Bilbo Baggins in J.R.R. Tolkien's
The Lord of the Rings

Resolving conflict collaboratively is a way of life. Some have likened it to learning a new language. It doesn't happen overnight. To venture beyond the familiar roles of the drama triangle requires compassion, courage, and perseverance.

Being a warrior of the heart

If I could bestow upon you one gift for your journey, it would be that of a "warrior mindset." Not the warrior we commonly associate with an aggressive hero (or murderous villain, depending which side we're on), but a "warrior of the heart."

I first heard the term "warrior of the heart" from Danaan Parry. His book of the same name is a "handbook for conflict resolution" that guides us in the inner work required to become effective peacemakers in the world. He drew on the Buddhist tradition of a warrior as "one who has the courage to know oneself." Knowing oneself includes facing our dark side or "shadow" — our inner villain. Danaan also refers to the Tibetan definition of a warrior as "one who faces one's own fear," willing to venture outside one's comfort zone. Both traditions see the path of the warrior as a journey within.

Danaan also talks of the Yaqui Indian concept of the warrior as one who brings newness to the tribe. The warrior ventures beyond the "tonal" (the known, the common reality) into the "nagual" (the unknown or unexplored reality). It is in the nagual that learning occurs and newness is found. Warriors of the heart are willing to leave the comfort of the drama triangle, fully experience the conflict, and explore new possibilities. As warriors, we demonstrate the courage to confront ourselves, including the parts we do not want to acknowledge — our fear, our pain, our self-righteousness.

While everyone's journey will be unique, we can learn from those who have gone before. To this end, I've shared below some lessons learned by my friends and colleagues on their journeys. All of them have integrated this approach into their daily lives rather than using it just while they are mediating or training. They have ventured into the nagual to change lifelong habits and patterns of dealing with conflict. I'm sure I speak for them when I say that none of us claims perfection. We've all had embarrassing moments when we have "lost it" or reverted to defensive or positional behavior despite being experienced professionals — prompting many a friend, spouse, and child to "helpfully" ask, "You do this for a living?!" I hope the following tips guide and inspire you on your journey.

The inner work

OBSERVING OURSELVES

> In conflict, our subconscious often triggers automatic reactions. To develop new responses, try spending a week simply observing yourself. Notice how you feel, what you think, and how you respond in conversation and especially in conflict. Avoid judging yourself, especially when you respond defensively. Instead of criticizing yourself, simply notice ("Wow, I really got triggered there"). When we let go of judgment, we no longer need to defend or justify ourselves. We create

room for curiosity and opportunities for learning. We can shed automatic reactions and deliberately choose more productive responses in conflict.

— *Donna Soules, mediator/trainer*

CLEANING UP OUR OWN ACT

Somewhere along this journey, I realized that the most important conflict resolution work we can do is to clean up our own act. In my experience, most conflict is "intrapersonal," that is, it lies within ourselves and has nothing at all to do with the other person. Even if we manage ourselves and our own emotions effectively, there will clearly be problems to solve and differences to deal with. But we are increasingly less likely to be triggered, to be reactive, or to contribute to the negativity in conflict as we continue to do our ongoing personal "cleanup" work. A life's journey, for sure!

— *Jill Schroder, mediator/meditator/mom*

RECOGNIZING THE IMPULSE

I've come to recognize in myself a defensive impulse that rises when I hear something that triggers me. I experience this impulse as a living thing trying to get out of me — a surge of energy that urges me to immediately challenge the other person to straighten them out. If unchecked, this impulse drives me to play the hero and to marshal impressive, but counterproductive, intellectual arguments and defensive reactions. Needless to say, these responses have not served me well in resolving conflict. Being aware of this feeling helps dissipate the urge to defend and allows me to go down a more productive road.

— *Gordon White, mediator/trainer*

PREVENTING EMOTIONAL HIJACKING

Our fears in conflict and frequently trigger emotions that may "hijack" us and render us ineffective. In exploring my own fears in conflict, I learned that in the face of someone adamantly telling me "the way it was," I felt helpless (and tended to shut down). I developed some self-talk that allowed me to deplane before being emotionally hijacked. By telling myself, "Breathe, I can handle this, get curious," I stayed present and focused in many situations in which I would previously have reacted unproductively.

So examine your triggers and ask yourself, "What do I fear?" From there, you will be able to create self-talk to reassure yourself in the moment to tap into your strength in the face of that fear.

— *Terry Harris, mediator/lawyer*

PAYING ATTENTION TO EMOTIONAL SIGNALS

For me, the key to applying these skills was to pay attention to my emotions. When I sensed that I was uncomfortable, frustrated, or upset in a situation, I used the feeling as a signal to step back and ask myself, "What's going on here?" Instead of simply repeating old patterns, I created a moment of calm in which I could observe what was happening and choose how to respond.

I remember waiting for a table at a local restaurant with my dad. I sat down in the nearest chair; he walked across the waiting area and sat in a distant chair. Conversation was impossible. I began to take it personally and a familiar internal tape started playing. It said, "You don't matter. And here's proof — even your own dad doesn't want to have anything to do with you." I was tempted to sarcastically ask, "Could you possibly sit any further away?" but I was able to pay attention to that emotional surge and forced myself to pause for a moment.

In this moment, I shifted my judgment and self-loathing to curiosity and asked him, "How did you reach the decision to sit in that chair?" He snapped out of his reverie, contemplated my question, and responded that, to him, it looked like the most comfortable. He was oblivious to the distance between us and certainly didn't intend his seat selection as a statement of any disregard for me. It was just dad being dad. His simple explanation allowed me to let go of my old tape and enjoy a pleasant dinner with him.

— *Keith Barker, coach emeritus/trainer/mediator*

WRITING YOURSELF A SCRIPT

One of the most helpful things I did was to create a self-talk script to replace my gremlins. I picked a particular situation in which I found myself triggered by my supervisor's constant use of the word "but" in conversations with me. To avoid reacting, I told myself, "Breathe. She's trying to tell me her needs. Listen for them. Be curious. This will pass." I repeated this mantra over and over until I was able to genuinely respond productively to her in conversation. Although she didn't change, our working relationship did.

— *Raj Dhasi, mediator/trainer/coach*

PROBING MY INNER RESISTANCE

I found the concepts of positions and interests have aided me tremendously in addressing my internal conflicts. When I find myself adopting a strong point of view or feeling resistant, I ask myself, "What's important to me about this?" For example, when I joined a tennis club some years ago I resisted playing on Court 1 (the spectator court) and encouraged my playing partners to go to one of the more private courts. When I examined my reaction, I realized that I was not only self-conscious as a beginner but also embarrassed that I wore knee braces as a result of five operations. My self-esteem was being pounded. When I peeled the onion far enough about what was bugging me, I was able to put my resistance aside to the point that I now prefer playing on Court 1.

By identifying my underlying needs and assessing their importance, I am able to make better and more deliberate choices in my life.

— *Ed Jackson, chartered accountant/mediator/trainer*

BUILDING A FOUNDATION OF VALUES

I found it invaluable to develop a clear sense of my basic values and beliefs. This allowed me to better understand why certain people, words, and situations triggered my emotions. In developing this clarity, I have to focus on the here and now — what my values are at this time in my life, rather than what I may think they *should* be. We need to lay this foundation before engaging in conflict, for we are unlikely to be able to sort this out with someone "in our face" and challenging us.

This reflection is a life's work, though over time I've gained clarity and associated my values more and more closely with a sense of well-being. Colleagues refer to this as "centering" or "getting in tune with oneself." Fortunately, the pilgrimage to Tibet is optional in this work.

— *Tim Langdon, conflict resolution coach*

JOURNEYING INWARD

What began as an exploration of conflict resolution turned into a journey of self-exploration. It had a dramatic impact on my life as friend, partner, and parent. The skills, the knowledge, and most importantly the self-awareness gave me the tools and courage to become more objective when confronted or in conflict.

This was best illustrated by my relationship with one of my daughters. We had developed a pattern of locking horns — hostility and anger (villain daughter) against indignation and self-righteousness (victim me). Doors would be slammed and insults hurled until the sound of U2 deafened me ("Turn that music down at once!"). During a Thanksgiving visit from my older son, my daughter interrupted our conversation to demand gas money for a friend. I was already feeling tired, stressed, and financially fragile. I raced up anger mountain so high it felt like Everest. This incurred a further barrage of insults. My son, likely wondering why he came home again, stepped into the hero role and tried to calm us down.

Then something shifted in me. I stepped outside the drama long enough to ask myself, "What is going on here? Why are we doing this?" As I slowed down inside, I remembered that I had promised gas money to my daughter's friend for all the driving she did. I admitted there she was right and that I had promised the money. I also told her that we were not going to resolve the issue by hurling insults at each other. "Could we discuss this?" I asked. My daughter paused, perhaps shocked by my failure to respond to the script we had created for ourselves over the years. She accepted my offer to sit down and talk it through, and before long each apologized for our harsh words. My son watched with mouth agape.

When my daughter and I were able to change how we communicated in that one incident, we changed the longstanding dynamic of confrontation and therefore our relationship. Though we still have challenges, we approach them more respectfully and more productively.

— *Jane Roberts, trainer/coach/mediator*

Active curiosity

STAY CURIOUS ABOUT THEIR BARBS

Significant for me was a shift from defensiveness to curiosity. I worked hard to "step outside myself" in the face of verbal darts from another person. This allowed me to recognize that their volleys were in fact defensive behavior and to wonder about what triggered their reaction. Understanding their behavior helped me deal with the real issue and not get sidetracked by personal attacks. So if I could recommend but one characteristic to embrace, it would be *curiosity*.

— *Derm McNulty, mediator/trainer/coach*

PUT YOUR OWN MOVIE ON PAUSE

I believe the most powerful skill to transform confrontation into cooperation is paraphrasing, in its broadest sense. When we can restate someone's story, including their words and emotions, we can dramatically shift the nature of the conversation. If we can put our own movie on pause for a minute and paraphrase their movie, a number of things happen: emotions defuse, assumptions are clarified, curiosity is fostered, and, eventually, understanding is built.

— *Jill Schroder, mediator/meditator/mom*

Focusing on specific skills

ONE A DAY

Most importantly, I made a deliberate decision to incorporate these skills into my life. To do so, I picked a skill to practice each day and used it at least five times in conversation. Monday was open question day and I consciously asked at least five open questions of people I was with, even when I had to force myself to be curious. Tuesday was listening day and I would practice paraphrasing or empathy with whomever I came across. Wednesdays were for pausing — I deliberately slowed my conversations and paused between sentences to allow room for silence. Over time, I managed to replace my old habits with ones that facilitated understanding and communication.

— *Raj Dhasi, mediator/trainer/coach*

TRAINING YOUR EAR

I liken learning conflict resolution skills to learning music. Along the way, we need to develop an "ear" for the skills we want to employ. I developed my ear by picking one skill each day on which to focus (paraphrasing, empathy, "I" statements, for example). I not only used these skills myself but also listened and looked for them in conversation, on television, in radio interviews, and even when reading a book or newspaper. I forced myself to listen more deeply by writing down examples of the "skill of the day." Like a musician who develops an ear for various sounds and instruments, I practiced to familiarize myself with the skills and make it easier to use them in conflict.

— *Donna Soules, mediator/trainer*

KEEPING IT ON THE FRONT BURNER

To keep conflict resolution front and center in my daily life, I've developed an ear for communication skills and an eye for conflict. I listen as top-notch interviewers on radio use questions to deepen understanding. When I observe others in conflict, I use them as case studies to determine where things went off the rails and how communication skills could have been applied. With stress levels in the workplace, I find no shortage of conflict from which to learn.

— *Clare Connolly, mediator/trainer*

CREATIVE WAYS TO PRACTICE

To integrate my conflict resolution skills, I practiced continuously. I would pick a skill each week and use it everywhere, especially with my family. Because they knew me so well, they provided direct and immediate feedback, especially when they didn't perceive me as genuine ("Did you take another course, Mom?"). I could also tell from their reaction when my skills were becoming more natural. As a break from the intimacy of family, I would turn to the anonymity of television, where I played off soap opera characters to practice my empathy and open questions.

Most importantly, I was willing to jump in and try it. I made a lot of "mistakes," but was gentle with myself, learned from them, and tried again.

— *Nancy Baker, mediator/trainer/mom*

THE CONFLICT PUZZLE

I now approach each conflict as a fascinating challenge. I generally take it less personally and actually enjoy strategizing how to best meet my needs and theirs. I don't want to trivialize conflict by saying it's "like a game," though I see it as a complex puzzle that is challenging, yet no longer overwhelming. Maybe more like the *New York Times* crossword puzzle. The first time you look at Sunday's puzzle it seems impossibly difficult. However, by working through a few easier Monday puzzles, then you're ready for Tuesday. Before you know it, Friday's puzzle seems pretty easy and you can't believe that you ever found Sunday's so overwhelming.

— *Roy Johnson, mediator/psychotherapist*

Changing the dance
Do something differently

In conflict, I try to do just one thing differently. This is particularly helpful with people who know me well enough for us to have developed unproductive patterns in communication. When I respond differently, even once, I change the pattern and cause us to develop new, more productive ways to communicate. And if I don't respond to their attempts to draw me back to our old ways, they will be forced to find a different approach.

For example, I was having problems getting a response from a contractor. My telephone messages asking him for detailed information went unanswered. Even in my frustration, I forced myself to consider what he might be thinking. I suspected that he saw my desire for detail as picky and even mistrusting. Old habits told me to avoid the conversation I knew I needed to have with him. Instead, the next time I saw him, I invited him to tell me if there is anything I say or do that ticks him off, because I'd rather deal with it now than have it build and lead to serious mix-ups. He smirked a bit self-consciously and said, "Good idea." The next day, he wrote down the information I needed and was very open to discussing the details of the job. By confronting the problem instead of avoiding it, I changed our unproductive pattern and opened communication between us for the rest of the project.

So just do *something* differently — anything — before you have a chance to think too much about it. And acknowledge yourself for doing things differently, even if they don't work out the way you hoped.

— *Ron Monk, mediator/trainer*

YOU CAN ALWAYS GO BACK

I found it freeing to know that in most conflicts I could go back and try again if I chose. I didn't have to get it right every time. This eased my anxiety and let me be more real when conflict arose. For example, I served on a board with a woman who was always late. When I learned about assertive statements, I worked carefully at framing one and delivered it. She scoffed. I let it be. At the next meeting, I took another shot, did some paraphrasing of what she said in response, and let it be. Next time around, I had another go. By then, I didn't care much what she did. I was very pleased with having given it a good effort even though she didn't change her behavior. I don't know what she is doing now, but I'll bet she's not on time!

Because I gave it my best shot, I felt better about myself and was able to step back and examine my own position. As I did, I thought, "Well, what do you know? Maybe I *am* a little anal about time! After all, this is the West Coast." That was a nice thing, too. I think when we are able to use these skills, we just soften up some, toward ourselves as well as others. I had many interests around time, but the fact was that I was clinging to the position that "we ought to start on time." It was illuminating.

— *Anon., lifelong conflict resolution student*

IF AT FIRST YOU DON'T SUCCEED …

I learn the most from conflicts that don't go the way I hoped. Even though I know what I *should* do, emotions and old habits sometimes get the better of me. I revert to old, unproductive patterns, despite my best intentions. When I step back and examine these situations, they are ripe for learning.

I can often apply that learning immediately. I recently butted heads with a colleague about how to approach a project. Within seconds my hard-earned skills evaporated as I dug in and defended my approach. The other person reciprocated and our mutual frustration grew. When I was driving home later, the knot in my stomach reminded me how I had lapsed into a confrontational approach. That evening, I asked myself why I dug in and what was important to me about the project. I strategized a more productive approach and put it into action the next morning. I told my colleague that our last meeting hadn't gone the way I wanted and I invited him to explain why he felt so strongly about his approach. Once he felt I understood him, he was willing to listen to my perspective. Before long, we reached a solution that left us feeling satisfied and on the same page. My inner perfectionist is relieved to know I can always go back and try a different approach.

— *Clare Connolly, mediator/trainer*

BLAH, BLAH, BLAH

Understanding conflict resolution from various courses was easy; applying it in the moment was a challenge. I remember an incident with an ex-girlfriend who remained a close friend. The previous day I had done something that ticked her off. Her irritation festered overnight and the following day, while we were driving home from work together, she confronted me over my transgression. In a flash, I realized I could use my conflict resolution skills. (This was a novel experience, for in the past I came to such a realization only after the fact.) This was quickly followed by a second, more sobering realization — I didn't *want* to use my skills. So I watched myself lapse into my familiar role in our pattern of attack, defend, blame, and justify.

And then something shifted inside and I heard myself saying to her, "This isn't getting us anywhere. I guess I better try to listen." My frustration then overrode my best intentions and I literally said, "So what you're trying to say is blah, blah, blah." This was obviously not a classic paraphrase, but it did appeal to her sense of humor and broke the pattern. Her sarcastic, "Well, now I really feel understood" was even tinged with amusement. I tried again and replaced my flip "blah, blah, blah" with an accurate summary of her concerns. She looked surprised. "That's pretty much it," she acknowledged and then, very easily, encapsulated my concerns. From there we were able to identify and constructively discuss what had happened the previous day.

Even though my initial attempt to paraphrase got sidetracked by emotion, it served to let her know that I was doing my best to understand. Since she wanted to be understood, she cut me some slack until I got it right.

— *Keith Barker, coach emeritus/trainer/mediator*

DON'T BE AFRAID TO MAKE A MESS

After over 15 years of professional conflict resolution, I would advise people new to this approach to "ignore perfection." It's annoying and unrealistic. Conflict is supposed to be messy. If the clashing of opposing interests is too neat and tidy, there's something that hasn't surfaced yet. Let yourself get dirty. Then help each other clean it up.

— *Roy Johnson, mediator/psychotherapist*

SHIFTING FOCUS

One of the best bits of advice I ever got about conflict came from my Scout leader over 30 years ago. During a winter backpacking trip he told me, "If your feet are cold, put on a hat." It worked. Although I was wearing warm boots and socks, putting on a hat kept the heat from escaping and warmed my whole body. One thing about conflict I learned from this is that sometimes we must shift focus from what is hidden to what is in the open. For example, when I am struggling to uncover a seemingly elusive solution, I stop chasing the solution and ask, "What is obvious about the problem?" Or, when I am mediating and find myself directing all the communication, I stop talking. Letting my clients fill that empty space is like saying to them, "If your feet are cold, put on a hat." It works.

— *Terry Neiman, mediator/coach*

TAKING RISKS AND TRUSTING YOUR GUT

Learning conflict resolution skills does not elevate us to sainthood or perfection. I give myself permission to be human — to feel, get angry, have feelings and make mistakes. This allows me to be myself rather than what I or others think I should be. When I trust my instinct and engage my heart as well as my head, I bring both creativity and integrity to conflict resolution.

— *Jory Faibish, certified mediator/trainer/architect*

EXPERIMENTING

As part of a study of conflict styles two years ago, I asked my 12th grade Peace and Development students to experiment with different conflict styles and record the results in their journals. I explained that the exercise was intended to allow them to experience alternatives to their "automatic pilot" responses to conflict. I encouraged each of them to choose a close relationship (parent, sibling, boyfriend/girlfriend) and to consciously choose a different response the next time they felt emotionally triggered. In other words, if they tended to avoid or accommodate (flight) then they were to engage around the issue by confronting or collaborating. If they tended to react competitively (fight), they were to see what happened when they accommodated or collaborated instead.

. I really didn't expect much and doubted whether they would take the assignment seriously. But when I read their journals three weeks later, I discovered that many of my students had profound experiences through this simple (but not easy) exercise. My subsequent classes have been given the same assignment and in reading more than 70 journal entries over the past two years, I have yet to find a student who did not report exceptional learning when they made a deliberate choice as to how to respond to an emotional trigger. Many learned about themselves in conflict. Others created an opportunity to talk about conflict openly and productively with the other person (often for the first time in the relationship). Others felt heard for the first time. And always the relationship was enriched.

— *Lloyd Kornelsen, teacher/trainer*

BITE-SIZED PIECES

Conflict resolution involves building relationships and trust. It takes time to shift the energy of conflict in a more positive direction. Don't expect to be able to resolve serious conflicts or the sources of conflict all at once. Think of conflict resolution as a process and give it time.

Shortly after taking conflict resolution training, I learned this lesson the hard way when I attempted to "collaborate" with a cousin who was staying in our home and driving everyone crazy. I sat him down at the kitchen table and completely overpowered him by trying to deal with all the issues at once. The immediate problem was solved as he moved out the next day. He soon sent me a scathing letter and we were in a full-blown conflict. The repair work then began, and it was several years before our relationship was mended.

— *Sally Campbell, mediator/trainer*

Don't go it alone

ASK FOR SUPPORT

When I first started taking the conflict resolution program at the Justice Institute, I practiced with my spouse and close friends. I explained I was trying to do things differently and asked them for feedback about how they experienced my efforts. As a result, my husband learned the skills very quickly and seems like a natural. I, on the other hand, am still practicing! As I became more comfortable with the skills, I was able to use my own words and so a collaborative approach felt less contrived. I do, however, continue to ask for feedback from others when things don't seem to be working well. They are usually more than willing to suggest positive alternatives.

— *Pam White, director of the Centre for Conflict Resolution, Justice Institute of B.C.*

BUDDY UP

Having the support of a friend or colleague continues to be key for me. When I was learning the skills, I found people to practice with. Even now, for what I expect to be challenging negotiations I prepare with the help of a buddy. I may role-play the conflict to understand what might trigger me, or simply talk it through with a colleague to help sift through and organize my thoughts.

I find it especially helpful to talk about situations after the fact with someone who understands conflict resolution. It helps me reflect on what worked well and why, and on what I could have done differently.

— *Jory Faibish, certified mediator/trainer/architect*

TACT ADVISORS

I see myself as collaborative and direct: I identify the problem, canvass those involved for their suggestions, and get on with what needs to be done. When I took a course in conflict resolution, I realized that some people found my directness intimidating. Yet even with this awareness and my newfound skills, I still struggled to find a way to work effectively with these people. Sometimes they would either react defensively to my presentation instead of looking at the proposal itself. Other times, they would seemingly agree with my suggestions, allowing the hero in me to charge off and implement my solution. In time, however, their unspoken concerns would surface as they participated only half-heartedly or actively undermined the "agreed" plan.

These challenges led me to assemble a team of "tact advisors" to serve as my sounding board. They help me ensure that my overall approach makes sense and that I present it in a way that encourages the other person to express themselves. We may even role-play difficult situations to prepare me for the real thing. When I'm ready to engage the other person, I initiate the discussion through a medium I can control — voice mail or e-mail. That way I can articulate my thoughts and set the stage for productive discussion. Face-to-face conversations can still be challenging, but my tact advisors serve as the "angel on my shoulder," reminding me to "shut up and listen." When I heed their advice, I create the space for the other person to put their concerns forward so we can truly collaborate.

— Gloria Hamade, human resources manager

Other tips

KEEP YOUR SENSE OF HUMOR

The anger and resentment that accompany unresolved conflict drain a lot of energy. Remember that most interpersonal conflict is not life-threatening. In some cases, we can use humor to relieve tension, lighten up, and let go of our negative feelings.

This lesson was vividly brought home to me when my husband was angry about some minor matter and was storming about, gesticulating in a very dramatic way, full of feeling. Our then two-year-old son entered the room, took one look at him, and burst out laughing. My husband was so startled by this response that he too started to laugh at himself and the absurdity of the situation. The tension immediately dissipated, along with his anger. (This approach is not recommended for those over two years of age.)

— Sally Campbell, mediator/trainer

A TIME AND A PLACE FOR COLLABORATION

I believe that collaboration, like any other tool or approach, is situational. In many situations, collaboration may not be appropriate, or even possible. I try hard to stay clear about when I am actually collaborating and when I am not.

— Pam White, director of the Centre for Conflict Resolution, Justice Institute of B.C.

INVEST IN RELATIONSHIP

The shift that made the biggest difference for me in applying conflict resolution in my life was around how I saw conflict. Historically, I saw conflict and differences as something negative. Instead, I began to view them as an opportunity to build a more productive, collaborative relationship. In one instance, the landlord of the building that housed my counseling office was very perturbed about the impact my clients might have on other tenants. After curbing my impulse to defend myself and show him the error of his views, I spoke with him at length on a couple of occasions. During those conversations, I remained patient and curious about his concerns and got to the heart of his story. He was able to express his concerns and explain how he had been burned in the past. As he realized I understood his story and experience, his voice calmed. He no longer felt the need to hammer home his point as he no longer saw me as the enemy. He then was willing to listen to my perspective and ultimately we negotiated a trial period that grew into a longer-term solution that worked for us both.

At first I wondered about the time and energy I had expended in my early telephone conversations with the angry landlord. I came to realize that it was one of the best investments of time I could have made. The time and cost for relocating my office would have been a great hassle. Also, my future interactions with him went very smoothly, in large part because of the respect I earned when I validated his concerns.

— *Gordon White, mediator/trainer*

PRACTICE, DON'T PREACH

When I first stumbled onto the notion of accountability in lieu of blame, the concept immediately made sense

to me. Developing the mindset and skills of self-respon-
sibility was a greater challenge.

Instead of trying to tell others how they should
behave, I focused on practicing accountability. I
attempted to model the behaviors that would move me
beyond the drama triangle into the circle of resolution
and found that as I abandoned my familiar roles, others
joined me in moving toward collaboration.

— *Neil Godin, team-building trainer/facilitator*

DO NO HARM

When I experience conflict, I consciously reflect on the
situation, analyze my reaction and the reasons for it,
then determine what I will do, or do differently next
time. (Even though the exact situation may never happen again, something similar almost certainly will.) I
ask myself whether this situation warrants a response
and, if so, what? A philosophy I learned as a victim/
offender mediator is that there should be "no more
harm." The best decision I can make is one that takes
care of my needs (lightens my burden) and inflicts no
harm on the other person.

— *Pam Penner, mediator/trainer/coach/consultant*

RESPECT ALL LIVING THINGS

The Buddhist wonder at the miracle of life in all forms
has helped me immensely in conflict resolution.
Though it may sound weird, I found it helpful to develop the habit of respect for all life: human, animal, and
plant. After all, if I can respect a bug, it isn't so hard to
respect even a person who behaves very badly.

— *Margaretha Hoek, mediator/trainer*

As these tips show, the work of conflict resolution is simple but far from easy. Yet the joy that comes from self-discovery and the rewards of understanding and relationship stir a passion in those of us who have adopted this approach in our lives. After a while, the journey becomes the reward.

As you embark on your own journey to apply the concepts and skills outlined in this book, I offer my heartfelt support and encouragement. And if, years down the road, you have forgotten the details of the book, remember to "stay curious."

Enjoy your travels.

The Road goes ever on and on
Out from the door where it began.
Now far ahead the Road has gone,
Let others follow it who can!
Let them a journey new begin ....

— J.R.R. Tolkien, *The Lord of the Rings*

Resources

Further reading

Beer, Jennifer E. with Eileen Stief. *The Mediator's Handbook*. New Society Publishers, 1997.

Cloke, Kenneth and Joan Goldsmith. *Resolving Conflicts at Work: A Complete Guide for Everyone on the Job*. Jossey-Bass, 2000.

Faber, Adele and Elaine Mazlish. *How to Talk So Kids Will Listen and Listen So Kids Will Talk*. Avon Books, 1999.

Kaner, Sam, with Lenny Lind, Catherine Toldi, Sarah Fisk and Duane Berger. *The Facilitator's Guide to Participatory Decision-Making*. New Society Publishers, 1997.

LeBaron, Michelle. *Bridging Troubled Waters: Conflict Resolution from the Heart*. Jossey-Bass, 2002.

MacDonald, Margaret Read. *Peace Tales: World Folktales to Talk About*. Linnet Books, 1992.

Mayer, Bernard. *The Dynamics of Conflict Resolution: A Practitioner's Guide*. Jossey-Bass, 2000.

Scieszka, Jon. *The True Story of the Three Little Pigs*. Puffin, 1996.

Stone, Douglas, Bruce Patton, and Sheila Heen. *Difficult Conversations: How to Discuss What Matters Most*. Penguin, 2000.

Tannen, Deborah. *You Just Don't Understand: Women and Men in Conversation*. Harper Collins, 2001.

Ury, William. *Getting Past No: Negotiating Your Way from Confrontation to Cooperation*. Bantam Books, 1991.

Whitehouse, Elaine and Warwick Pudney. *A Volcano in my Tummy: Helping Children Handle Anger*. New Society Publishers, 1996.

Winslade, John and Gerald Monk. *Narrative Mediation: A New Approach to Conflict Resolution*. Jossey-Bass, 2000.

Organizations

Centre for Conflict Resolution
Justice Institute of B.C.
715 McBride Boulevard
New Westminster, B.C. V3L 5T4
Phone: 604-528-5608 (Greater Vancouver)
Toll free: 1-888-799-0801 (across Canada)
Website: www.jibc.bc.ca/ccr/

The center has offered skill-based, experiential training in conflict resolution for over twenty years.

The Earthstewards Network
Box 10697
Bainbridge Island, WA 98110
Phone: 206-842-7986
Fax: 206-842-8918
Publishing: 800-561-2909
Website: www.earthstewards.org

The network was founded by Danaan Parry, and continues his work throughout the world. It is a nonprofit organization with a mission to "take bold action for conflict transformation and the creation of positive relationships bridging boundaries of gender, age, culture, race, nations and beliefs." The Earthstewards offer many opportunities to put theory into practice.

Bibliography

Carson, Richard David. *Taming Your Gremlin: A Surprisingly Simple Method for Getting Out of Your Own Way.* Rev. ed. Quill, 2003. Originally published as *Taming Your Gremlin: A Guide to Enjoying Yourself.* Perennial Library, 1983.

Covey, Stephen R. *Seven Habits of Highly Effective People: Powerful Lessons in Personal Change.* Free Press, 1989.

Crum, Thomas F. *The Magic of Conflict: Turning a Life of Work into a Work of Art*. Simon & Schuster, 1987.

Fisher, Roger, Bruce Patton, and William Ury. *Getting to Yes: Negotiating Agreement Without Giving In*. 2nd ed. Penguin, 1991.

Parry, Danaan. *Warriors of the Heart*. 5th ed. Earthstewards Network, 1997.

Scott, Susan. *Fierce Conversations: Achieving Success at Work and in Life, One Conversation at a Time*. Viking, 2002.

Harper and Associates
5693 Eglinton Street
Burnaby, BC V5G 2B5
Phone: 604-299-3201

Website: www.garyharper.ca

- Workshops
- Keynote Speaker

INDEX

ABOUT THE AUTHOR

Gary Harper is a consultant, writer, and trainer who specializes in management training and business communications.

Through his unique blend of experience as a personal injury lawyer, general manager, insurance regulator and retail store owner, he learned the value of clear, effective communication.

In 1991 he completed the Conflict Resolution Certificate Program offered by the Justice Institution and the Commercial Mediation program through the Vancouver Centre for Commercial Disputes.

He designed and conducted a variety of workshops on communication skills and conflict resolution for managers, shop stewards, municipal employees, adjusters, and bylaw enforcement officers, among others. He has trained for the Justice Institute of B. C., I.C.B.C., the Workers' Compensation Board, B. C. Transit, Revenue Canada, and the University of British Columbia and its Women's Resource Centre.

His interest in the archetypal characters of the "drama triangle" of conflict lead him to develop a course entitled "Once Upon a Conflict". He uses the concept to illustrate how we can move beyond confrontation towards collaboration.

He is known for his high-energy and humour and for the ability to foster a positive, supportive learning environment. He believes people learn best when they are actively engaged and having fun.

He can be contacted at <www.gary harper.ca>.

If you have enjoyed *The Joy of Conflict Resolution*,
you might also enjoy other

BOOKS TO BUILD A NEW SOCIETY

Our books provide positive solutions for people who want to
make a difference. We specialize in:

**Environment and Justice • Conscientious Commerce
Sustainable Living • Ecological Design and Planning
Natural Building & Appropriate Technology • New Forestry
Educational and Parenting Resources • Nonviolence
Progressive Leadership • Resistance and Community**

New Society Publishers

ENVIRONMENTAL BENEFITS STATEMENT

New Society Publishers has chosen to produce this book on recycled paper made with
100% post consumer waste, processed chlorine free, and old growth free.

For every 5,000 books printed, New Society saves the following resources:[1]

25	Trees
2,283	Pounds of Solid Waste
2,512	Gallons of Water
3,276	Kilowatt Hours of Electricity
4,150	Pounds of Greenhouse Gases
18	Pounds of HAPs, VOCs, and AOX Combined
6	Cubic Yards of Landfill Space

[1]Environmental benefits are calculated based on research done by the Environmental Defense Fund and
other members of the Paper Task Force who study the environmental impacts of the paper industry.

For more information on this environmental benefits statement, or to inquire about environmentally
friendly papers, please contact New Leaf Paper – info@newleafpaper.com Tel: 888 • 989 • 5323.

For a full list of NSP's titles, please call **1-800-567-6772** *or check out our web site at:*

www.newsociety.com

NEW SOCIETY PUBLISHERS